Moving Past Personal Crises

Paul R. Shaffer

authorHOUSE®

AuthorHouse™
1663 Liberty Drive
Bloomington, IN 47403
www.authorhouse.com
Phone: 1 (800) 839-8640

Published by AuthorHouse 11/19/2018

ISBN: 978-1-5462-6877-2 (sc)
ISBN: 978-1-5462-6878-9 (hc)
ISBN: 978-1-5462-6876-5 (e)

Library of Congress Control Number: 2018913640

Contents

Contents

Acknowledgements

Thanks to Barb Swartz for the last-minute design suggestions, and to Jeff Seiler for his continuing editorial skills.

Also, my thanks to Debbie Anderson-Medves, Connie Sanders-Sybert, and Diane Reid-Lyon for taking the time to do a preliminary read-through of my work.

Foreword

Life is made up of both good and bad, and not always in equal measure. We are better prepared for crises once we've accepted that life is going to be difficult at times, adjusting our expectations to better fit reality. Experiencing personal crises can be completely normal, even predictable, but it's just as important to know that they're also survivable and, sometimes, even preventable.

Crises can be self-inflicted due to poor choices or a chaotic personality, but many times they are just circumstantial – life happening. Whatever the reason for their occurrence, while they can derail us from the life that we were living, they can also be a transformative catalyst for positive change and growth. Good can come out of bad.

If we're learning to better deal with them, it means, in part: 1) raising our awareness of what makes us more susceptible to experiencing a personal crisis, 2) knowing what tools are available to either help prevent, or help move us through, those difficult periods, and then 3) getting more proficient with using those tools when they're needed. This book will be focusing on the first two. The practice piece is up to you.

◆　◆　◆

Beyond my thirty-some years of being a professional counselor and working with clients in crisis, this book is also a personal one for me. Currently at the age of 55, one could safely predict that I'd have gone through at least one personal crisis in my life by this point, and the truth would be that, so far, I've gone through two.

My first crisis was while going through a marital separation back in my mid-30's. The second was only two years ago after both of my parents had passed, and my daughter had grown up and moved out. I was also having to accept visible signs of my own aging, and I had just lost my best friend of eight years.

After writing several self-help books, mostly on relationships, I was pretty content, up to that point, that I had said my piece. However, after my own recent crisis, and then witnessing friends and family going through some struggles of their own, I felt led to write down a few more things I had learned over the years – both professionally and personally.

Because each person is unique, I can predict that some things in this book will work for you and some things will not. Rarely does any one tool work every time, so you need to: 1) have a variety of tools to choose from, 2) take the time to practice them so you know how to use them effectively, and 3) not throw a tool away prematurely just because it didn't work for you the first time you tried it.

Some people latch on more easily to thinking strategies, while others are more doers. I find that the best approach is knowing how to do both, so I will be discussing both in the chapters ahead.

Let's get to it.

Chapter 1
Emotional Pain

At the most fundamental level, when it comes to personal crises, we need to have a healthy understanding of the role that emotional pain plays in both a negative and positive direction. For most people who struggle with the stress, anxiety, or depression that comes from being in crisis (or leads to a crisis), the desire is to get rid of the pain altogether. Peace, for them, is defined by an absence of negative emotion. However, while that can be true to some degree, it isn't actually a good thing to get rid of emotional pain altogether since it actually serves a healthy purpose when in the proper amount.

Most emotions that have been labeled as negative still have necessary positive components. *Anger*, if steered in an appropriate direction and expressed in non-destructive ways, gives us the strength to stand up for ourselves and make necessary changes. *Guilt* can move us to accept responsibility for our mistakes and help us take steps to correct our path back to something that restores our self-respect.

Healthy *anxiety* usually occurs in situations where we need to be paying attention to something that's a potential threat, something that we need to learn to do better at or be better prepared for, or something that needs to be fixed or finished.

Problematic, or unhealthy, emotional pain is better measured by its extremes. It's an issue if there is too little of it when there needs to be some, and an issue when there's too much of it, leading us to feel overwhelmed (discomfort becomes distress). *The healthy in-between is the place where we both manage and take guidance from necessary emotional pain, rather than letting it go unexplored and it managing us.*

If I'm getting too close to the edge of a cliff, there needs to be a concerned voice in my head telling me to be careful. That's my self-preservation doing its job as it should. It becomes problematic if either 1) that voice starts screaming that I'm going to die, paralyzing me, or 2) if there is no inner voice at all, putting myself in unnecessary risk because I'm getting too close to a dangerous drop.

The discomfort that comes from emotional pain ideally motivates us to take positive action. If we fail to take appropriate action, we will be left with the continuing discomfort.

◆　◆　◆

On a similar note, our emotions that are usually labeled as positive can have negative connotations if they gravitate to the extremes. Being completely lost to *love* can also leave us blind in terms of our better judgment. And if we feel too *content* we may lose any desire for further self-improvement, or making a difference with our lives.

The positive feelings that come out of the high someone gets when they use drugs, or alcohol, or gamble, or overeat, or overspend, or over-exercise, can move them all the more quickly to becoming psychologically dependent on those things just to get by. They get lost in the destructive cycle because of the momentary positive emotional payoff.

While many expect happiness to be their natural state if their life is going well, and assess that something is falling short if they're not feeling it, happiness is actually a *peak* experience. It's not realistic to expect it to be a continuous state of being. If you're doing well, then a more realistic inner experience would be feeling good, content, or at peace.

◆　◆　◆

I will have clients complain of feeling anxious because they're in an anxious situation, or feeling depressed because they're in depressing circumstances. They will feel like something's wrong with them, but the fact that they're feeling the predictable emotional discomfort for their particular situation is to be expected. Their brain is responding as it should.

In part, they have to adjust their attitude about the pain that their emotions can create. If they see those feelings as simply their internal alarm system working properly, then it's no longer something dysfunctional. They need to respect the warnings and take a look at what needs to be done, if anything, about a potential problem.

If I'm feeling anxious about a speech I have to give, then I need to get more comfortable with the material I'm presenting so that I now have a greater degree of confidence about what I need to say.

If I'm stressed over my bills, I need to be responsible with my spending and being disciplined enough to follow a budget. If my income keeps falling short of my expenses, and it's not due to over-spending, then I may have to look for a better job.

If I'm feeling depressed over the loss of a loved one, I have to allow for the time that it takes to mourn my loss rather than try to rush through it.

If I'm distressed over my romantic relationship because we're drifting apart, then I need to again start doing the things that brought us together in the first place, looking at what steps need to be taken to restore the connection.

This is all common sense, but in the moment we are often: 1) too emotionally overwhelmed, 2) too close to the situation to see the logical way out, 3) don't want to have to do the work that's required to improve the situation, or 4) want immediate relief before we've actually done anything to get that relief.

I've known of several problem relationships where the counsel given by friends or family was to not worry about it – that things would just work themselves out. But, in reality, the couple needed to worry *more* if it would actually motivate them to finally make necessary changes.

In each of the situations I listed above, the emotional discomfort attached to the experience was normal and healthy. Emotions become problematic when we've taken the necessary steps to deal with our situation but the same degree of emotional discomfort persists or worsens. In those situations, our brain isn't accepting that we've done enough, even though we have.

Sometimes the problem is that there's nothing we can directly or immediately do about what's happened (or what is happening), so we have to either work towards acceptance, or figure out how to be okay with doing nothing for the time being (which is usually when having healthy distractions or other positive projects to focus on becomes important).

We'll talk about these problematic situations later in the book.

Situational, Clinical, and Chemical

Anxiety and depression, while having different clinical sub-categories, still share the same broad categories of situational, clinical and chemical.

Situational anxiety or depression is just that – we're in a particularly difficult situation and so we're feeling the predictable impact from it. Usually when the situation passes, or we come up with a decent solution for getting through it, the emotional discomfort lifts.

Clinical anxiety or depression is when the emotional discomfort is so significant in its frequency and severity that it's starting to interfere with our daily functioning – sleep, appetite, work, activity level, relationships, etc. Sometimes, what starts off as a situational issue can leave us emotionally stuck (even though the situation has passed), so it now becomes a potential clinical issue.

With either clinical anxiety or depression usually treatment is recommended – meaning counseling and possibly temporary medication management. These are considered mood disorders and, these days, are highly treatable.

Chemical disorders are when the cause of the emotional pain is biological, not psychological. This is when we feel emotional pain for no visible reason whatsoever, and positive circumstances and interventions don't seem to make a difference.

◆   ◆   ◆

Usually, even before attempting psychological treatment, it's a good idea to get a thorough physical in order to first make some medical rule-outs that might be causing the emotional issues. I have had cases where the real issue was a hormonal problem (such as with a hypo or hyper thyroid), or even a vitamin deficiency.

Back when I was a teen, I developed separation anxiety, not understanding that it was actually due to a physical issue. At the early age of 10, I started experiencing random heart palpitations that felt like a fish kicking in my chest, making me catch my breath and scaring the hell out of me. The first time this happened I was at summer camp, separated from my parents, and unable to see them until later in the week. When I was finally able to tell them, because I wasn't experiencing actual pain, they dismissed my symptoms, leaving me with unresolved feelings of dread.

A second incident occurred about a year later, when I was at Prince Gallitzin State Park for a sailboat race with my neighbors for the weekend. In the middle of the night, in the upper bunk of a cramped car trailer, the palpitations came back. Not really knowing how to process these fears as a child, I developed separation anxiety. Whenever I was to stay overnight at a friend's place, or my parents would go on a trip, I would get this overwhelming fear of something bad happening. I didn't make the connection until I was an adult that my separation anxiety came from those initial incidences with the palpitations.

As an adult I further learned that the palpitations were PVCs (which are common and not life-threatening) – so I had spent a lot of time worrying about nothing, and that much of the time the PVCs were due to just being dehydrated (I grew up in a family that didn't drink much water).

Medication

When is it appropriate to consider using medication to deal with emotional pain? Many people will see meds as a non-option. They may feel strongly that they need to get through their crisis on their own. However, while doing it on your own is the preferred path (because it can build greater self-confidence and better coping skills), it's not always realistic. Sometimes, medication is necessary.

The primary *benefits* of using medications are: 1) the resulting emotional and physical relief, 2) the stabilizing effect they have on your mood so normal functioning returns – such as your ability to sleep, eat and think, and 3) restoring your ability to focus so that you can now learn and apply better tools to cope.

The *downside* of using medications include: 1) the potential side effects, 2) the time that it takes having to try different meds, or a combination of meds, until you find a fit for your particular chemistry, 3) the time it takes for the medication to reach its maximum benefit, 4) the potential for abuse of the medication, and 5) the possibility of becoming dependent on the drug.

There is a difference between becoming physically dependent on a drug (where our body craves it), and becoming psychologically dependent, where it's just in our head that we think we can't deal without it. Many medications do not carry the risk of dependency, and, even for those that do, some people are more susceptible than others.

For someone whose mood issues are due to a chemical disorder, where their body's chemistry is off and is not going to self-correct, medication is a necessary intervention and will likely need to be a long-term intervention.

However, for someone with either situational or clinical mood issues, using meds is an "it depends". Usually what it depends on is how severe their current symptoms are. But even then, for them, med management is not a long-term solution, it's a short-term solution. The solution it's providing is getting the individual stabilized to the degree that they can put some better tools and supports in place so that when they go off the medication they can now cope without it.

That's usually the deciding line I use with my clients. If their distress is so great that, while they can have a good session, they can't retain any of it (or apply it) once they're out my door, then they need to be considering temporary medication. It's just to help get them back to where they're functioning well enough that they can actually use the tools that I'm giving them.

Prolonging the Pain

I am frequently amazed at some of the people who show up for counseling as to how long it's taken many of them to get there. Often, they have been in incredibly dysfunctional circumstances for years, but they stubbornly persist in trying to solve it on their own, or ignore it, hoping that it will fix itself.

Many times, in these situations, there is an underlying desire to avoid pain and discomfort – not just of the problem itself but also the discomfort of having to openly talk about the problem, and having to admit failure at solving it. However, in the end *avoidance just prolongs the pain and discomfort*. If they had just allowed themselves to acknowledge the crisis, and that they needed help, things could have gotten better a lot sooner.

That's not to say that solving problems on your own is always a bad choice. If you're actively pursuing solutions, adding new tools to your toolbox, then go for it. Self-education, such as through reading books like this, taking workshops, attending support groups, talking to experienced friends or family, can all be positive, effective steps to gaining the information and knowledge that we need. But, for many, "solving it on your own" translates to trying to fix a problem with only the tools that they already possess, which may have already proven to be insufficient.

Often, as adults, we are still using the same set of coping tools that we practiced using as kids, however, those tools usually don't work as well, if at all, in the adult world. Crises tend to force us to upgrade our toolboxes, to find better, more mature, means of dealing with life and its challenges. And that's okay because better tools are available.

Bullet Points:

- **Emotional pain can be normal, necessary and even healthy. It's only a problem in the extremes – too little or too much.**

- **Anxiety and depression fall into similar categories: situational, clinical, and chemical.**

- **For situational crises, medication is sometimes necessary, but it is only a short-term solution, allowing us the time to restore our focus and put better tools in place.**

- **Mental health is sometimes defined by how we manage, or fail to manage, our emotional pain. We can repress it, work through it, or overly indulge in it. Working through it is the healthy choice, with the best outcomes.**

Discussion Questions:

1. Do you tend to feel that *any* kind of emotional discomfort is unhealthy or bad? Do you expect that you should be stress-free in life, or are you okay with some degree of stress? What is the difference between healthy and unhealthy emotional pain?

2. If you've had a personal crisis in the past or present, would you say that the emotional distress you felt at the time was more situational, clinical or chemical?

3. Other than the present, have there been any times in your life when your emotional pain rose to unhealthy levels? If so, what did you do to get it back under control? Do you still use any of those strategies to manage your pain now? Do you have better strategies in place now than you did when you were younger?

Chapter 2
Legitimate Needs

Part of dealing with emotional distress is through better understanding the underlying unmet needs that are typically contributing to that distress.

We all have three core needs in life: security, significance and fun. *Security* is about feeling like we've got control over the direction of our lives, that we are safe, and that we belong. *Significance* is about feeling valued and that our existence matters. *Fun* is about quality of life and freedom of choice.[1]

Needs are always legitimate. By definition, we *need* them. We can only deny them for so long before some degree of anxiety, depression or crisis sets in. Needs, by themselves, are not the problem. *The problems are always in how we go about trying to get them met.*

Similarly, the problem isn't that we experience emotional pain. The problem is how we go about handling that pain, or not handling it – whether we're adequately satisfying the underlying legitimate need that's possibly being threatened.

Part of the problem with the solutions we find to relieve emotional pain is that, because emotions are often short-sighted, many of the solutions we come up with are only short-term fixes that can create bigger problems in the long term.

---

[1] Some would question why I don't include love as a need, but love is a combination of both security and significance. If I feel loved, I feel both valued and emotionally secure in that relationship.

For example, a couple with poor conflict resolution skills chooses to remain silent rather than raise an issue and risk the discomfort of conflict. They've prevented a fight in the moment, but, by not getting practice at talking things out, their issues are now stockpiling. Their security need is being temporarily met by maintaining the peace, but it's ultimately threatening the long-term security of the relationship by not really resolving the problems.

In addition, we will find ways to temporarily, artificially, satisfy our underlying need, creating the illusion that the problem's been solved when it hasn't.

For example, the person who uses TV to distract themselves from an unsatisfying life, may indulge to the degree that now they're just watching other people's lives, adventures and accomplishments rather than spending that time creating a meaningful life of their own. (The underlying legitimate need in this situation is both significance and fun.)

Need versus Needy

There is a difference between having needs versus being needy. Men, in particular, are often raised to be self-reliant, so they will sometimes have difficulty in acknowledging a need to their partner (or friends), because part of being a man, for them, is not needing anything from anyone. Acknowledging need, for them, is seen as being weak or selfish, but they are really mistaking legitimate need for being needy.

In a crisis, men will tend to self-isolate – which does not make things better, it makes things worse. They fail to recognize that we lose perspective in the midst of a crisis, and we need others to help us see more clearly.

There is often a one-sided relational dynamic to this where one person is more than happy to meet the needs of another, but won't identify any needs of their own. They fail to recognize that, in close relationships, most of us want to feel needed in some way. By keeping their needs to themselves, they are keeping everyone else at an emotional distance, preventing others from being able to contribute to the relationship.

Since we connect with others through our own humanity, if we can't acknowledge our own human wants, needs, feelings or desires, then others will have a hard time finding something to connect to with us.

"Being needy" is when we are trying to get too much from someone or something that we should be doing for ourselves. For instance, people that suffer from low self-esteem will often be overly dependent on the praises of others, because their own self-praise holds little or no worth. And, even then, they may tend to dismiss or minimize the praise they do get, even though it's what they want to hear.

By putting ourselves beyond needing others, we can create the illusion for ourselves that we are without need. Yet, that, in itself, is need-fulfilling behavior. I feel significant through my independence and self-sufficiency. I remain secure by feeling in control of my life, not allowing myself to rely on anyone else or let anyone in. So I am projecting this image of competency to the world, but it can actually be dysfunctional relationally.

Independence can be an act of self-protection, a sometimes unconscious way to avoid vulnerability and being hurt. If your history has been that people let you down, it makes sense that you would have trust issues. But you still might need to take a look at your expectations of others to see if they're realistic (because nobody's perfect), and possibly do a better job of picking trustworthy friends, because they do exist.

Independence may be well-intended, not wanting to burden others, but it can still be problematic, contributing to becoming self-absorbed and cut off from true relationships. During hard times, we all need as many healthy supports as we can get. For those who have a difficult time acknowledging their need to others, they have to recognize that, rather than weakness, it takes a lot of strength to be vulnerable enough to say that you need something – even if it's just to talk, or get advice, or wanting to hang out. You're not being a burden to others by sharing your pain, or needing their company, you're allowing them to be a friend – hopefully the same thing you would want them to come to you for.

Sometimes, though, acknowledging need is just an issue of semantics. She asks him to identify a personal need of her, but he doesn't feel strongly enough about anything to the degree that he would label it as a need. (This may actually indicate that she's already satisfying his needs, if none come to mind for him.) But, if instead she had asked him for his preferences or desires, what he would *like* rather than need, it might be a much easier conversation for him to participate in.

◆　◆　◆

In most crises, emotional pain is usually experienced as feelings of stress, anxiety, or depression – sometimes a combination of all three. As they relate to our three core needs: anxiety is more frequently connected to the need for security, depression is typically related to significance, and stress is often due to a lack of fun.

Anxiety, Control and Security

Anxious thoughts typically regard the unknowns or the things we feel that we don't have full control over, which directly impacts our need for security. Because the extremes are always the easiest to see, when we are feeling insecure we typically then gravitate to the extremes of either overcontrol or undercontrol.

Overcontrol is when we try to take too much control when we shouldn't. Being a bully would be an example of both over-control and insecurity. *Undercontrol* is when we don't take enough control when we should, such as with procrastination.

People who have control issues usually struggle with *both* undercontrol and overcontrol. And usually they have underlying anxiety, even if they can't admit it or see it.

Often, overcontrol and undercontrol exist in the same situation. For example, the parent/partner who micromanages everyone's lives in the home might be over-compensating for not having a life of their own outside of being a parent or partner. They are overly controlling others, but not taking enough control of themselves. These situations create an illusion of being "in control", but that person might actually be out of control, especially if they can never step back and stop being that person.

The overly performing executive might feel good about their achievements, status or wealth, but their satisfaction with their current success is usually short-lived. This is because they are performance-driven, so it's all about what comes next, rather than fully enjoying what's already been accomplished. Their constant need to prove themselves, to be doing something, never establishes any lasting sense of self-worth, so they are usually very uncomfortable with being still or without a task to keep them occupied. They appear to be very much in control of their lives, but it's what drives them that is actually in control.

For reactive couples (those who keep reacting to each other's reactions), though on the surface there is an obvious control struggle, in reality each person is giving up their control. I say this because, by waiting on the other person to do the right thing first, they are practicing helplessness. The truth is that the only true control they have in the relationship is over themselves, and yet they keep letting their partner dictate what they do next based on the next thing the partner says or does. They may feel anxious over the future of the relationship (which they should), but they have stopped doing the positive things that would steer the relationship back on a positive course because they are overly focused on the wrong person – the one they can only influence, not control.

Usually we do have some degree of control even in the worst situations, but we may overlook it or fail to take advantage of it. Instead, we stay overly focused on what is beyond our control, or overly doubt our ability to handle what is still in our control.

Depression, Helplessness and Significance

While anxiety can be immediate, depression tends to develop over time (unless it's due to a sudden unexpected significant loss). The longer someone remains in a negative situation, or fosters a negative mindset, the more they run the risk of experiencing depression. If depression reaches clinical levels, there is often a sense of hopelessness or helplessness imbedded in their thoughts. They're not seeing a way out, or don't feel like they have the energy to get there.

Rather than the overcontrol/undercontrol dynamic of the anxious, depressed individuals typically lean just towards undercontrol. They aren't taking control when they should. Their depressed feelings dictate more depressed behavior. While they may feel like they don't have the energy to "take control", they fail to grasp that you have to expend energy to create energy. They are typically waiting for their feelings to shift rather than doing the things that would help that shift occur.

When our need for significance has taken a serious hit, it can be experienced in several different forms. We may not feel appreciated or valued by those that we work for or by those that we care about – that our existence doesn't matter to anyone other than us. We may feel that we're not doing anything meaningful with our lives. We may feel that we either have no purpose, or have lost the purpose that we had. We may feel helpless to change our circumstances. In these situations, it makes perfect sense that someone would be feeling depressed.

Similar to anxiety, the depressed individual needs to take into consideration the cause of the depression, question the possible thought distortions that they might be buying into (which I'll talk about in Chapter 8), and restore their focus to better satisfying their underlying needs. In other words, retake control of what's still in their control. If the depression is due to personal loss, and it's something that can't be regained (such as the loss of a loved one), then the work is about moving towards acceptance of that loss and gradually reconnecting with life.

Realistically, sometimes moving out of depression can be a longer path than moving out of anxiety. It usually takes longer to get there, and it might take longer to get back out. Some of that depends on whether the rebuilding work is just about correcting thinking errors, which can be a relatively quick and simple process, or if the issue goes deeper than that. When you're talking about a loss of feeling valued, or having meaning and purpose, those are progressive projects and don't happen overnight. So patience, persistence, and realistic expectations become very important.

I'll spend more time on managing problematic feelings, with a focus on depression, in Chapter 9.

Stress, Lifestyle and Fun

Stress usually comes from feeling like the current demands on us are too great, too many, or uninvited. We're struggling to keep up, or with finding the motivation to keep up.

While we can have a life that is balanced and still feel stress, one of the first things to look at when stress is becoming problematic is our lifestyle and how much we may be creating our own stress by:

- taking on too much
- not setting a realistic pace for ourselves
- being too disorganized
- having poor time management
- not knowing how to say "no"
- not knowing how to delegate responsibility
- not being able to separate our work from our personal life
- not having a life outside of work
- not turning to our partner, family, or friends, for necessary support and distraction
- not having any activities that reenergize us
- not knowing how to, or taking the time to, relax

One symptom of being overly stressed is that everything is now being taken too seriously. Perspective has been lost. There is a lack of humor and playfulness. There is an absence of fun. The more stressed we are, the less we are typically taking time to enjoy life.

Coping with stress, just as with anxiety and depression, is about taking back control of our life. In this instance, it's about reducing the demands on us where we can, learning relaxation skills, doing a better job of balancing, and restoring perspective by putting more of a priority on taking the time to stop and smell the roses.

Ultimately, we are trying to learn to say "yes" to our underlying needs, since they're always legitimate, but doing so in ways that still respect moderation and balance. And we are trying to stay with solutions that are healthy, in that they are effective, meaningful and lasting.[2]

Bullet Points:

- **We all have three core needs: security, significance and fun.**

- **If our needs go unmet long enough, we will begin to experience crisis.**

- **When security is threatened, we will feel anxious.**

- **When significance is lacking, we will feel depressed.**

- **When fun is absent, we will become more stressed.**

- **Needs are always legitimate. The problems come from how we attempt to meet, or not meet, those needs.**

- **One approach to managing stress, anxiety and depression is viewing them as control issues. While we're trying to take back what control we still have in those situations, we are trying to avoid the extremes of overcontrol and undercontrol.**

---

[2] This is also true for our relationships. With friends, family and partners, one of the biggest keys to getting along is remembering to always place a value on their underlying needs. Sometimes we can't say "yes" to the exact way that they're asking us to meet those needs, but our focus needs to remain on what ways we can, rather than how we can't.

Discussion Questions:

1. Of your three core needs (security, significance, and fun), currently which needs are the most satisfied and which are the most starved? If one or more are being neglected, what needs to happen in order to better satisfy the ones that are going unmet?

2. Does how you go about trying to get your needs met actually work for both the long-term as well as the short-term? In other words, is how you're satisfying your needs in the present likely to cost you further down the road, or get you closer to where you ultimately want to go?

3. Do you tend to struggle more with overcontrol, undercontrol, or do you think you practice a nice balance? If you've got a partner, what do they say about you, regarding that? If you need better balance with that, what would that look like?

Chapter 3
Balance

One of the biggest determining factors for whether or not we are inviting a crisis-driven life has to do with how well we maintain balanced priorities in our personal life. For the crisis-driven, they essentially depend on a crisis occurring in order to force them to take positive action or make necessary change:

The procrastinator relies on the stress of the pending deadline to stir them to movement.

The people pleaser takes on too many obligations until they are overwhelmed, forcing them to have to let go of something.

The undisciplined spouse shapes their partner to have to chronically complain or issue ultimatums before they'll step up and do what they promised.

The overeater ignores self-care until health issues start to occur.

These are all crisis-driven scenarios, where people are practicing dependency on increased emotional discomfort in order to inspire healthier behavior.

◆　◆　◆

Even for those who are not crisis-driven and practice better balance, at the point a stressor (be it circumstance, thought, event or person) occurs, their tendency may be to allow the stressor to become their primary focus.

It makes perfect sense that, if a problem presents itself, then we would want to figure out its solution. But, if the problem persists, then the longer we overly focus on just the problem, distracted from everything else, the more likely it is that we will fall out of balance and that the problem will now have other problems to keep it company.

One of the most important things to remember regarding personal crises is that *the quickest way out of a crisis is to restore overall balance.*

I wrote about balanced priorities in both my book on dating as well as my book on marriage because it's that important. Often, we will be experiencing stress in one area of our life, but fail to realize that it's all of the other out-of-balance areas that are actually adding to it.

One of the initial steps in addressing a crisis is sorting out what's still in our control, and all of the most common life priorities fall under that label – things that we still can do something about (at least to a degree).

The active priorities in our life can usually be whittled down to the following categories:

- job
- romantic partner
- kids
- social relationships
- relatives/in-laws
- hobbies and interests
- health and exercise
- spiritual walk

We may tend to look at these priorities as a hierarchy where there's supposed to be a particular order – one always coming first, another second, etc. But the reality is that these are juggling balls and it's all about how we split our attention between them. Each needs to come first at some point, before the others, if we are to keep them all in play. If we overly focus on any one for too long, then there is a chance that others are going to get dropped.

Because we only have so much time, ideally we learn how to multitask between the priorities: sharing exercise time with our partner or kids, involving friends in a particular hobby, etc. The better we are at doing it, the more we will feel like we have an actual functional life.

Job and Relational Roles

As far as time investment, our job typically comes first, since it's where our income is coming from – our financial security. But it's also where we will often get our sense of identity, our self-worth, recognition, status, sense of success, and feelings of accomplishment. It can become so need-fulfilling that we may not feel like we need to have anything else in our life outside of our work.

Yet, if work becomes everything and our job becomes problematic, or we even lose it, we will likely go into immediate crisis because there is nothing else to sustain us.

For those workaholics who become overly concerned about financial security, having enough for their retirement, often they won't take the time to live life in the present because they're so focused on the future. Yet they fail to realize that there is no guarantee that they will live long enough to spend what they have saved, and are missing out on the opportunities to live life along the way.

For men raised in traditional role-based homes where the man's only role in life was to be the primary breadwinner, if the man was holding down a job and not abusing his partner, he was doing all that was expected of him. So it was easy for everything to be just about the job, and it was the wife's role to support that.

Similarly, for the woman raised in a traditional role-based home, her expected job, once married, was to take care of her man, her kids and their house. Her identity was all about being a wife and a mother, without any priority attached to developing any sense of self. (Her "job", if not married, was to find a man.)

21

Both of those traditional roles were out of balance.

In more recent generations, relationship roles have become blurred between who does what, with many of the roles now being shared. However, whether a marriage practices traditional roles or more modern roles, there is still the problem that occurs when any relationship becomes just about the roles.

Fulfilling the roles is what gets things done. It's the "to-do's" that are getting checked off – the chores, the obligations, the work. Yet what brings couples together in the first place, and keeps them together, is not usually just doing the work together, it's also the connection.

The connection consists of the intentional fun that the couple has together, the physical/emotional/spiritual intimacy that they create and maintain, and developing their shared passions. If the connection takes a backseat to the roles for long enough, the relationship will wither. The couple can be doing everything that they think they're supposed to be doing, but the relationship can still die if the connection gets significantly neglected.

Past whatever commitment was made, the connection is what motivates the couple to continue to fulfill their roles. Without the connection, everything becomes just work. In which case, the romantic relationship turns into either just a work relationship, or a roommate relationship.

Partner

Our romantic partner, ideally, provides a degree of emotional security, respect, self-worth, and belonging. They can also be a source of pleasure, excitement and fun.

During the in-love stage, it's predictable to see individuals make their partner the center of their universe, overlooking friends and everything else in the process. Because their relational needs are being satisfied, they won't feel like they need anyone else in their life, but it masks the fact that their life is now out of balance.

What happens if the relationship becomes challenging, or even fails? Hello, crisis.

There is a balancing act that every romantic relationship has to figure out. As their relationship progresses and gets past the initial infatuation, if the relationship is healthy then it should support and encourage each other having balance in their lives, not distract them from it.

Typically, just with the passing of time alone, as familiarity and routine sets in, it's easy for each partner's attention to drift back to all of the other priorities, but at the risk of the relationship (especially the connection) being taken for granted. So now it's out of balance in the other direction.

Whoever is the more relational will typically become the voice for the relationship, but this is really a role that needs to continue to be shared between partners. Each needs to continue to provide input as to what's working and what needs work if it's going to continue to be a joint project. If it's just left to one partner, that partner will often come to resent being the only one looking out for "us", and the other will resent what they come to see as the other's chronic complaining.

In the dating world, there is sometimes the tendency for one person to chronically practice making it all about the other person in order to show how much they care, suppressing their own opinion (and need) in the process. So, the relationship starts out with only one voice. At some point, though, the less opinionated partner will need to add their own voice if the relationship is going to be an actual relationship.

◆　◆　◆

For those out of balance, there is a tendency to approach relationships out of neediness, maybe not even realizing it, simply because there is so little else in their life that is need-fulfilling. For them, it's very hard to assess the people that they're in relationships with because their own need will distort what they see in them. And it will be harder for them to end any unhealthy relationships because it means they will be consciously choosing to walk away from one of the few things in their life that they're getting something out of, no matter how poorly.

Kids

In this day and age, there is often a tendency when raising kids to make our world revolve around them – their schedules, their activities, and their happiness. And then we end up with entitled children who think it's supposed to be all about them, because that's how we raised them.

Our kids need to have a better sense that mom and dad have needs, too, that sometimes come before their own. They need to be raised with the awareness that there's a bigger world out there with many other people who have the same rights and needs as they do.

Parents, while needing to be responsible for meeting their child's food, shelter and educational needs, and showing them that they're loved, *aren't* responsible for their child's happiness. The child's happiness is up to the child to find for themselves. Of course we *want* our children to be happy, but when we take it on as our obligation, the child comes to expect that if they're not happy then it's the parent's fault. The child learns how to manipulate this to get whatever they want, and the parent ends up becoming a constant servant to the child.

Too many parents will avoid necessary consequences for a child's misbehavior because they can't bear their child's emotional discomfort. The entitled child's mentality is that if they feel hurt by what the parent did or said to discipline them, then the parent is being mean or unloving. To prove this isn't true, the parent will attempt to soothe the child through words or rewards, which sabotages the necessary discomfort that the child needed to experience as a consequence of their actions. As a result, the parent ends up reinforcing the child's belief that a loving parent only focuses on the positive, not the negative.

In part, we practice balanced priorities as a way to model a balanced lifestyle for our children, and their place in all of it.

Balanced *parenting* practices both praise for a child's positive choices and firm, loving accountability for the not-so-positive.

Social

Typically, a social life is more present when we're in our twenties and thirties. As we marry (or our friends marry), and then kids come into the picture (or our friends have them), the focus on maintaining adult friendships tends to drift. Whoever is more relational (usually the woman) will likely put a higher priority on keeping friendships alive. However, that can't control for how those friends may still drift from us, distracted by their own lives.

When we're younger, friendships usually develop just through continued exposure to others – through school, work, social functions, church, etc. Many of those friendships aren't conscious choices we've made but just how things develop with time and familiarity.

As we get older, our time becomes more valuable, because there's less of it to go around. We start making more intentional choices about what we're going to do with that time and with whom we're going to do it. Ideally, we take a closer look at the quality of our friendships and the quality of our friends – weeding out the takers from the givers. The healthier friends are the ones who are more positive, mature, balanced, supportive, and (ideally) wise. They are those who can be counted on to be there for us in hard times, as well as the good. Hopefully, these are the same qualities that we are developing in ourselves.

Because good friends are hard to come by, sometimes we have to search for such friendships, accepting that there will be more that aren't good fits than those that are. We also have to become more intentional about deepening our friendships – having better conversations, allowing for quality time and opening up. Otherwise, we can have some good potential friendships that never reach their potential.

For couples, it means finding other healthy couples to do things with. Not only can this help with creating a support network for such things as raising kids, it increases the likelihood that the couple will get out more often – having a life outside of the home. If that other couple is a healthy one, they may also be able to provide emotional support and wise guidance during difficult times.

The problem with a lack of social supports is that, *without friends, all of our relational needs will now fall on our partner (if we have one) and that's too much for any one person to bear.*

Relatives & In-laws

In previous generations, family was much more of a community experience than it is today in America. There are still some cultures within America that place a high value on it, but the majority of families today are disconnected from the aunts and uncles, grandparents and cousins. They often don't live in the same area, and don't maintain consistent communication. As a result, there is the loss of both a potentially positive support system and a sense of generational roots. We lose a layer of identity because we are disconnected from our own extended family, as well as from our family history.

Often, with aging, reconnecting with extended family becomes more important. But, maintaining those family and in-law relationships often depends on how functional the people are. Dysfunctional relatives can disrupt one's life and current relationships. If boundaries are poor, or they are chaotic individuals, you are now allowing that chaos into your own life.

If it's your partner's extended family that continues to negatively intervene in your relationship, and your partner wants them to remain in their life, then it becomes a delicate situation – and a potential crisis. Setting respectful boundaries becomes important in preserving and safeguarding your own family.

For some, friends are closer, and more reliable, than family. For others, "blood is thicker than water".

When it comes to balance, we are looking at both maintaining, deepening and healing the relationships we have with extended family – especially with those that are the healthiest. That's not to say we ignore the unhealthy, especially if they are open to becoming healthier. But we also need to be realistic and self-protecting of ourselves and our immediate family about who we let in.

For some of us, we are more susceptible to crises in the present because of unresolved emotional wounds we received from family in the past. If at all possible, rather than letting our pride, our pain, or a stubborn nature keep our hurts festering through the years, shaping our lives in unhealthy ways, we need to consider modeling a better path and attempt resolution where resolution is possible.

◆　◆　◆

When I first got out of graduate school, I worked with a comprehensive care center that did group therapy for a senior home. While for those professionals that came before us that meant playing bingo and handing out coffee, my colleague and I wanted to be a little more creative and so we would take the seniors out for drives into the surrounding countryside in the company van. It was amazing how those quiet, reclusive souls, when exposed to that external stimulation, would start to come to life, recalling meaningful stories from their childhoods – whatever the passing landmarks stirred in their memory.

Because of that experience, it made it very real to me how much knowledge and history is potentially lost with each passing generation when we remain so self-absorbed with our own lives that we never take the time to learn about our parents' and their parents' histories. When my own mom and dad entered their late 60's, I sat each down and interviewed them on video, documenting their life stories both for myself, my daughter and future generations.

Don't take family for granted, and don't forget the potential wisdom and support they can provide during difficult times.

Hobbies

Hobbies and personal interests are typically about fun, accomplishments, and identity. They help balance the work.

If there are *no* hobbies, everything becomes work. *Too much* time with hobbies; and the work isn't getting done.

Ideally, we're choosing hobbies or interests that are authentic fits for us – things that resonate with who we are. The better the hobby fit, the more likely it will become a personal passion – something we can pursue for the rest of our lives.

Health

Health maintenance (diet and exercise) is huge when it comes to its interactive relationship with anxiety, stress and depression. On a very basic level, both help inoculate us against the impact of stress while also supporting our sense of self-worth and self-confidence.

Exercise tends to be one of the very best ways to manage anxiety, even better than medication because it's our body's natural chemicals that are being released to regulate how we feel.

Part of the secret to maintaining an exercise routine is to choose a form of exercise that we actually enjoy (again, finding an authentic fit). If we choose a form of exercise that we hate, but still force ourselves to do, we are just finding another thing to stress over.

Both diet and exercise are about maintaining a higher quality of life throughout your life, a practice in self-discipline, healthy self-love, and usually provide the most visible evidence of you taking care of you.

Spiritual

As far as spiritual walk, the final chapter of this book will spend more time on it. While it can be connected to a particular religion, it doesn't have to be. It's how we look beyond ourselves and the everyday, how we struggle with meaning and overall purpose in life, as well as how we develop a personal faith or philosophy (in whatever form that takes). It can be a direct support of our need for security and significance.

The older we get, there is a tendency to focus on just two or three of these priorities due to time limitations, and a tendency to gravitate to either what's most comfortable for us, what's easiest, or what is making the most visible demands. Unintentionally, we can then become overly dependent on those two or three remaining active priorities meeting *all* of our personal needs.

Sometimes, when there are too many demands, we can go for great lengths of time so distracted trying to meet those demands that we fail to realize that our own needs have gone unmet for quite a while. In those cases, we've been unintentionally practicing self-neglect.

Yes, there will always be dry periods in life when our needs will not be met the way we would like them to, where circumstances may be interfering with certain priorities being satisfied the way they used to be. And that's okay, for a time. Those are usually the transition periods in life – a new job, an injury, a move, kids, aging, etc. We can all manage temporarily with need deprivation when the situation demands it, but the priorities list is about, beyond the situation, intentionally keeping our lives well-rounded so that, when one area is suffering, we have other areas to keep us afloat.

For those with a balanced life, who have found an authentic fit for the majority of the priorities, every "category" that's being taken care of is an affirmation of who they are, what they like, what's important to them, what they believe and why they believe it. There is a very clear, consistent and well-rounded picture to their identity, rather than a shifting picture that changes, depending on who they're with or what's happening in their life. They are able to bring a complete person to their relationships because they have a clearer sense of self, and are less likely to create their own crises or fall into crisis when bad things happen.

◆　　◆　　◆

Every time I do individual work, I ask a client to do a priority exercise as their first homework assignment. It gives me a quick overview of what's most important to them, where the greatest demands are, and how in or out of balance they currently are. It also helps them to get a better perspective of themselves and where the work needs to be done.

At the core of it, in terms of managing stress, it helps them refocus on something they can control, rather than overly focusing on what's not in their control. (The actual exercise is included at the end of this chapter.)

Bullet Points:

- **Being crisis-driven means being dependent on crises (or significant emotional discomfort) to occur in order to force us to take necessary action or initiate change.**

- **The easiest way to avoid things building to a crisis, or move past a crisis, is to restore balance to our lives.**

- **Balance is reflected in how well we juggle our core priorities.**

Priority Exercise:

1. Take a sheet of paper and write down the different types of priorities in your life: job, partner, kids, friends and family (social), health (exercise and diet), interests/hobbies/fun, and spiritual (purpose/meaning in life/personal faith).

2. Now take a few minutes and think of where the majority of your time and attention is going. For the priorities that are getting the most attention, draw a larger circle around them. For the areas that are the

most neglected, draw a smaller circle. This is an easy visual to show where your energy needs to be going. You need to be subtracting time and effort from the larger circles and diverting them to the smaller ones.

3. Take some time to itemize the things you do for each particular category. By itemizing, you may find that it wasn't as much as you thought, or maybe it was more than you thought. If you want to get serious about it, you can even itemize the frequency of those activities and the amount of time that goes into each during a normal week. (If you're open to it, invite your partner's opinions as to the accuracy of your assessment.)

4. Now take a second sheet of paper, which will represent "your life in balance". Write down the same categories, but now itemize the things you could realistically start doing in the neglected areas that would restore some balance to the picture.

5. Now that you've identified what you could be doing, you need to make a specific plan for how you're actually going to *start* doing those things, in order for it to become a reality. That plan needs to start with the first simple steps that would lead into accomplishing the greater task. For instance, if one of the things you'd listed was to take an evening class, the first few steps might be to get a class listing, decide what evenings you have to work with, and decide from that listing what class you were interested in that fits with your available evening. The steps need to be small enough, and immediate enough, that you can start acting on them within the current week.

Depending on how easily distracted you are, you might want to continue to review the priority list on a weekly or monthly basis to measure your progress and keep yourself on track. If you *don't* have a specific plan, it probably will not happen; you'll just know that it *should* happen. The priority assessment serves as your own personal accountability system. It's what you can focus on at the start of the day to incorporate into your day, and/or what you review at the end of the day for how you did, and what you can do better at tomorrow.

Chapter 4
Information, Choice &
Locus of Control

So you recognize that some emotional pain is necessary at times, you've been putting more conscious effort into attending to your personal needs and the needs of others, and trying to do a better job at keeping your life priorities in better balance. Yet a situational crisis presents itself anyway. What are the initial steps to dealing with it?

Step #1: Get as much information as you can to better understand your situation.

When faced with a personal crisis, many will try to just not think about the stressful thoughts that come from it, but the reality is that usually when our brain keeps bringing something up it's looking for better answers. There may be an unknown that's stressing it and it wants to be able to fill in the blanks. There may have been an incident that we can't change in the present, but it keeps reviewing what could've been done differently in the past. Maybe it's trying to take something that was unacceptable and find a way to accept it.

If there's a potential threat, our brain's fight or flight center wants to know just how much of a threat it is. It wants a plan, in order to feel safe. If there is insufficient information, or no plan, our brain is not going to let us completely relax because, as far as it's concerned, the threat has not been sufficiently addressed.

Sometimes we do already have the information we need, or already have a plan to address the issue, but our brain doesn't like the answers, or isn't completely content with the plan because no plan covers every eventuality, but that's a different issue. Here, I'm looking at when the crisis *initially* occurs, before we have the information or the plan.

If someone has had their house broken into, and this is the first time that has ever happened to them, then they may now feel unsafe in their own home, develop sleep issues, become hypervigilant, and any number of other reactions. They need a plan as to how they're going to prevent this from happening again – such as purchasing a security system, getting a dog, etc. Just being able to do *something* can lower their feelings of helplessness and lack of control.

If someone's partner has just discovered an affair, the victim will naturally have a wealth of questions they need to have answered in order for them to understand what has happened and what needs to be done. They often get stuck on the "why's". If there are no answers, or insufficient answers, they remain in crisis. The added dilemma here is that, even if they are given sufficient information, they will often no longer feel like they can trust that information because they no longer trust the source of that information.

If a panic attack happens for the first time, catching someone totally by surprise, not knowing what's going on with their body, or how to handle it, is part of what escalates the panic. The more information they have about what happened, the "why", and what they can do to manage it in the future, the more likely the anxiety will ease as they learn to regain control over their body's reactivity.

◆　◆　◆

In some situations the problem is that it's not possible to know everything that we want to know in order to feel at peace.

If a couple is considering reconciliation, they may want guarantees on the front end that it's going to work before they are willing to emotionally reinvest. While, ideally, they've learned some better tools to reapproach the relationship (rather than just a changed attitude or renewed motivation), they will only truly get the evidence they need by attempting to reinvest and seeing if they are able.

A college graduate who is just starting their chosen career path may be riddled with doubt as to whether it's the right path or whether they will be successful, but it's only through actual experience that they will gain meaningful confidence with their own abilities, as well as find out if it was a good choice or not.

For these situations when the information cannot all be known in the present, people have to exercise patience and delayed gratification. They have to trust that they will get the information they need as time goes on. In the meantime, they will need to be focusing on just the work in front of them that will get them there – the only thing in their control at the moment.

The Worst-Case Scenario

Sometimes, even though our feared worst-case scenario may be unlikely, our brain won't let up until we've allowed ourselves to consider it. That is not to say that we should torture ourselves with it, but to think the "what if" through, past the imagined catastrophe.

I had a client a few years back who was looking at a possible short (several months) stay in jail for a pending charge. His crime was not premeditated, but an altercation between himself and a police officer that got out of control over a misunderstanding. Now, he was haunted by the possibilities of what could happen to him if he did go to jail, and feeling helpless that there was nothing he could do at this point to clear up the misunderstanding. I'd worked with the prison system for several years, doing groups and assessments, visiting inmates. In comparison, my client had never been in either a jail or a prison. While I didn't want to minimize the experience for him, I did want him to have more realistic expectations than the stereotypes of the places presented on TV and the movies. While jail and prison are not fun experiences, the reality is that, if that's where you are, then you learn to adjust to it. You learn the new routines, you learn to deal with boredom, you put in your time and you move on (depending on the length of your sentence). When I "normalized" the experience for him, he was able to let go of much of his anxiety over the worst-case scenario.

For the partner who feels stuck in their relationship, yet their worst-case scenario is divorce, they don't like where they are, but the alternative seems unbearable. While most of the immediate work might still be to focus on improving the current state of the relationship, sometimes the worst-case scenario still needs to be talked out, discussing the "if" of what divorce would look like if it were handled fairly and respectfully. This is tricky territory since it can set off the other partner's insecurities that divorce is actually happening, and, yes, it could make it more doable for the one afraid of divorce to now take that path. But, sometimes, what happens is that, because choice has been restored, to stay or to go, the feeling of being stuck is removed. And, so, the discomfort with staying is no longer so uncomfortable because it's back to a choice. After all, if we have a partner, most of us want to know that they are staying with us because they choose to, not because they felt like they had to.

Even when it comes to the worst-case scenario of death, with hospice care these days there can still be a peaceful ending without pain.

So, by filling in the blanks as much as possible with options for how we would handle the worst-case if it ever occurred, we're normalizing it to a degree. And by seeing that it's survivable, or at least doable, once we've mapped it out, it will often ease our concerns to more manageable proportions.

◆　◆　◆

The reality is that, even in some of the worst situations, once we're in them we still learn to adapt and survive, finding our way through. It's still painful, but we continue to live and, hopefully, learn from it.

At the same time, for those actually living out their worst-case scenario, it's natural for them to doubt their ability to adjust, especially if they've never gone through something like that before. However, the initial adjustment is still first gathering information by: 1) learning from others how they got through such situations, 2) getting educated through books, consultations, workshops or counseling that provide tools and strategies, and 3) paying attention to the information they're getting about themselves that the crisis is bringing out – what helps them have a better day and what makes things worse.

Step #2: Map out all of the potential choices, both good and bad, with the given information (identifying what's actually in your control to do).

When it comes to freedom to choose, let's talk about three different scenarios:

- those who have no choice

- those who have choices but don't like any of them

- those who have too many choices and don't know which one's the right one to make

Having the ability to still make choices gives us some degree of security even in the midst of crisis. It's certainly harder for those who feel like the choices have already been made for them.

For those going through a crisis due to a catastrophic event, an unexpected death of a loved one, or a critical mistake or circumstance that can't be undone, part of learning to move forward again is learning how to live with what happened (learning how to accept the seemingly unacceptable), and part of recovery is reconnecting with the choices you make in the present in going on from there. No, *you can't change what happened, but you can decide how you're going to handle it and go on*. Will you choose to let it totally derail you, or will you get back up and figure out how to reinvent yourself and your life?

I worked with DivorceCare for a few years, a support group for people going through both marital separations and divorce[3], and the people that had the hardest time moving through their separation were always the ones that had been left – where the choice had been made for them. Even if they agreed that the relationship hadn't been healthy anymore, it was more difficult for them because they weren't the ones who chose to end it. Predictably, I'd see them get stuck for a while trying to process what had happened, trying to rehash the relationship issues with the partner, and just having a hard time between working towards acceptance versus trying to regain control of what was happening.

For those where reconciliation didn't happen or wasn't successful, they would often enter into an uncomfortable limbo period. They had had a vision of their life going a particular way, and now that vision had been taken away. Until they came up with a new vision for their life (something revised for the current circumstances), they would have to learn to allow themselves to be okay with being in limbo for a while.

That new vision wouldn't be an overnight process. It would often come in steps, initially just looking at restoring balance, an opportunity to put their own life back together in possibly a healthier way, and then starting to explore where to go from there. As they reconnected with their choices in the present, and acted on bringing their new slowly-forming vision into reality, they would usually start to feel better and be more confident that they could successfully move on.

◆　◆　◆

---

[3] The name is a little misleading because DivorceCare is really designed more for the separated than the divorced, though it works with both. One of the benefits of support groups is that you get to see that there are others going through, and surviving, similar circumstances - effectively getting the message across that you are not alone. Support groups can provide both the community that you may be lacking, as well as the tools for dealing better with your circumstances.

Some people feel like they are in situations where they have no choice, but they still do.

For the person who feels stuck in their current job, seeing their life not going anywhere, they *could* quit, but then they'd have to deal with the insecurity of being without an income or benefits while trying to find another job. (Ideally, they'd be looking for other job options while continuing with what they currently had, so if they did find something it could be a transition that wouldn't require going without an income.)

Maybe they are aware of other available jobs but those jobs don't pay as well, or the benefits aren't as good as what they currently have, or are just not the type of work they think they'd like. But the reality is that there *are* other options, it's just that the other options aren't better than what they already have. The more accurate problem is that, because they don't see their other choices as good ones, they feel like there are no choices. However, *they are failing to take any satisfaction from, or give themselves credit for, making the best choice of the ones that exist.*

Consider the person who is still single when all of her friends are now married, and she would like to be married as well. She may feel like there's something wrong with her for not having a partner. She may feel like she has no options because all of her past and current prospects either fell short, or just weren't a good fit. But the reality is that she has had plenty of options, it's just that she didn't settle for any of them. Unless she was actually being too critical of the ones she rejected, she was doing the *healthy* thing by not settling. So nothing was wrong with her, she just had yet to find a good (not perfect) fit, and that isn't something that can be forced or is easy to come by. She should be giving herself credit for not settling, allowing herself to feel good about making the harder healthy choice.

Choosing to do the healthy thing does not always feel good, but that doesn't make it any less healthy. And many of the best choices require a degree of delayed gratification that can be very difficult to practice when we're feeling desperate.

Even good choices come at a cost; it's just that they're worth the price. Bad choices cost us more than they're worth.

◆　◆　◆

Sometimes the issue is that the existing positive options are going to require us to step out of our comfort zones, and maybe involve a degree of risk or the unknown. So it feels safer to stay with what we know. In such instances, we are still making a choice by choosing to do nothing.

Step #3: Sort out the good choices from the bad (the healthy from the unhealthy).

For those who are stuck because there are too many options, the issue may be that either there's not enough information yet to pick a path between the different options, or that they're holding out because they think there's only one right choice and they don't want to make the wrong one.

If it's about not having enough information, then we need to allow ourselves the time to gather more information in order to make a decent choice. On the other end, sometimes we already have more than enough information, but our insecurity convinces us that it's still not enough – so now we're just procrastinating.

For those that feel *every* choice has a right or wrong, they are creating unrealistic anxiety for themselves. While there are some clearly good and bad choices in life, there are just as many situations that are about trying to just make the best choice out of several potentially good ones.

Sometimes there is no "best", and sometimes there is no real right or wrong, we're just stressed because we think that there is. *Sometimes any choice can be the right one so long as you make the most of whatever choice you make.*

Living in Charlotte, North Carolina, many people come here because of all the job opportunities. And some, after making the move, will then proceed to go into crisis because they feel it was the wrong decision. They gave up all of their friends. They haven't found any new hobbies. Their old exercise routine has been disrupted. But there's nothing that says that they can't make new friends, restore old hobbies or find new ones, and join a new gym. Their choice to move wasn't a wrong one; they just weren't yet making the most of the choice they made. They expected it all just to work out rather than recognizing that it was going to require effort and patience on their part.

◆ ◆ ◆

To balance what I've been saying so far, you do need to be careful not to make big life-altering decisions when you're caught up in strong emotions, because feelings will distort your perception. For those choices, it's usually better to wait out the emotions, to see if there's consistency in your thinking in between the emotional waves if you're going to be able to feel the decision to act is a good one, and not have regrets later on.

Many people in the midst of crisis will make hasty changes driven by their emotional reactivity, but they have to be careful because what they might be doing is just adding new stressors to their life rather than lightening the load.

◆ ◆ ◆

One guide for helping people make choices has to do with whether or not the choice involves healthy or unhealthy love.

Unhealthy love is about doing what feels good in the moment, but is actually counter to what you want to accomplish for your future. For instance, he spends too much time in his hobbies, at the cost of his romantic relationship.

Healthy love is doing in the present what's consistent with your future health and wellbeing. For instance, maintaining that exercise routine because you want to have a certain quality of life when you get to your senior years.[4]

---

[4] This applies to relationships as well. If the couple is able to keep a focus on what is best for the future of their relationship (the *us*), rather than getting lost in self, they will make better personal choices because they are keeping the bigger picture in mind.

Locus of Control

In the midst of a personal crisis, the meanings and interpretations that we attach to what we're going through can make a very big difference, including how we look at the choices that are available to us. Attribution theory (Weiner) puts people in two camps. There are those who lean towards an internal locus of control and those with an external locus.

For those with an extreme *external* locus, everything that they do they see as being caused by something outside of themselves. Their partner made them angry. Their job is keeping them from happiness. Their kids are ruining their life. They do not take responsibility for either their emotions or their actions because something or someone else made them feel that or do that. But what they are actually practicing is another form of helplessness, giving up their inner control to outside influences.

The unhealthy payoff for keeping an external locus is that we remain untouchable if it's never our fault. We never have to apologize or take responsibility if there's always something, or someone, else to blame. But you can't really have a relationship with someone who is never willing to be held accountable. They stay protected, but they miss out on true intimacy, and an opportunity to grow in maturity.

For someone with an *internal* locus, their happiness, their success, their behavior and their feelings are all their own responsibility. Nobody makes them feel or do anything, because they recognize that it is their *choice* how they choose to respond rather than just instinctively react. The outside world and the people in it can certainly *influence* them, but that doesn't ultimately decide what they do with it. As a result, they are practicing healthy control.

If we have an internal locus and are in a relationship with a reactive partner, we are more likely to continue to be loving, *despite* the partner's reactivity, because we stay focused on being consistent with the healthy person that we desire to be in that situation. In doing so, we also retain our self-respect and, ideally, the partner is left with the weight of their own impulsive reactions. We don't ignore accountability for their negative behavior, but we are not adding our own bad behavior to the mix.

At the same time, an internal locus, if taken to an extreme, could become problematic if that meant we were taking too much credit for our personal successes or failures when other factors might have contributed to them as well. We might be making ourselves overly responsible for things that weren't really our responsibility.

So the ideal would be back to striving for a *balance* between an internal and external locus, where we could accurately identify and take responsibility for only what was truly our responsibility.

As it relates to crises, we are trying to take back personal control over our feelings and actions/choices, rather than practicing helplessness and letting our emotions, or the situation, dictate what we do. Neither are we holding ourselves responsible for situations that we didn't create.

While part of our concerns may be due to feeling like we *can't* control our own feelings at that point, we are lying to ourselves if we choose to believe that there's nothing we can do to regain control. There are always choices that we're making in the midst of crisis that we often fail to see, both good and bad.

◆　◆　◆

Locus of control can get misused. For instance, I had a client once say something intentionally hurtful to her partner. The partner then told her that she had made him feel hurt by her words, to which she replied defensively that, "I can't *make* you feel anything. You decide how you feel." While she thought that she was accurately citing a principle of locus of control, she was misapplying it by not taking personal responsibility for her intentional harm. If her partner had inappropriately reacted to what she said, while she shouldn't take full responsibility for his reaction, she should still have taken ownership that there was a more respectful way of initially expressing herself, and have attempted to do so.

Step #4: Stay with the choices that work best for you.

Having identified what the best options are in your current circumstance, you obviously have to act on those options if you want to see any benefit.

If your situation involves several different changes you can make to improve things, as you are taking actual steps, following through on your chosen options, pay attention to those choices that make the most difference for you. In other words, not all positive actions are equal. Some will resonate better with you than others, and these are the ones that can become your personal lifelines. For some, focusing on their relationships (or creating new ones) may give the most reward. For others, it may be finding a new personal passion. For others, it may not be an action but a shift in attitude, a different, healthier way of thinking.

Be thorough with exploring your new choices. Don't give up too quickly if a new path doesn't pan out immediately. For instance, if regular exercise is one of your positive new paths that you want to take, but you find that you hate the gym, don't give up on exercise. Find a form of exercise, or a better exercise environment, that works for you.

Bullet Points:

- **When we first experience a potential crisis, we need to ask ourselves if we already have enough information to truly understand the situation, or if we're just making some quick negative assumptions or projections. Often we are operating with only partial information. If we're lacking information, our first path is to seek more. Knowledge restores a healthy sense of control.**

- **We also need to identify what our choices are, because there are always choices, we may just not like some of them. Reconnecting with choice can restore a sense of freedom.**

- **How we learn to make good choices can usually be guided by knowing what healthy love looks like. If we're exercising** healthy love towards ourselves, then we're not focused on immediate gratification, or solely on what our emotions are pushing us to do, but what actually moves us closer to the healthy person we desire to be.

- **An external locus of control means that we view everything outside of ourselves as being responsible for the current state of our lives.**

- **An internal locus of control means that we take personal responsibility for our choices and our own happiness.**

- **A balanced locus of control is good at separating what is our responsibility and what is not.**

Discussion Questions:

1. Have you been in situations where a lack of information was part of what was stressing you out? How did you handle it? For your current stressors, do you have the information you need in order to know your options? If not, what's holding you back from getting the information you need?

2. Have any of your worst-case scenarios ever come true? Were they ever as bad as you imagined? If so, how did you survive them? Do you avoid thinking about worst-case scenarios because they're too stressful to consider? Do you understand the value in sometimes thinking them through?

3. Do you feel like you have options or do you feel stuck? Are there choices you could be making, it's just that, comparatively, they're not good ones? Are you able to give yourself credit for making the hard choices, even when having to choose between the lesser of two evils? If there are better choices for your situation, what's holding you back from making them? Do you get overwhelmed by having too many choices? If so, do you get that not every choice has a right or wrong attached?

4. Do you feel that you have more of an internal locus of control, an external locus of control, or a good balance? What does your partner, if you have one, say about that? If too external (to the degree that you're practicing helplessness), what would you need to do differently in order to shift it to more internal? If too internal (to the degree that you're overly controlling), what do you need to do to let go of some of that?

Chapter 5
Focus

While there is an internal or external locus, there is also an internal or external *focus*. The better skilled we are at being able to adjust that focus between internal and external, the easier it's going to be to move through a crisis.

For people who are more introverted, intellectual, or self-analytical, there tends to be more of a natural internal focus to their thoughts. This may make them more inclined to overthink situations, sometimes creating their own stress even when they're not in a stressful circumstance. Typically, their emotions are more likely to be kept inside rather than openly expressed unless something forces them to the surface.

For those who don't engage much in introspection, while a benefit to this is that they don't normally have issues with overanalyzing, the downside is that they are less prepared when a crisis occurs, as it forces them to become internally-focused. Since this is unfamiliar territory for them, they are often less equipped to know how to handle it.

When we experience stress, anxiety or depression, some degree of introspection is necessary in order to try to think things through and come up with some solutions for how we're going to move out of it. However, too much time in introspection and now introspection is becoming part of the problem. We are becoming internally stuck.

Past the point that we have done necessary introspection, we need to be able to switch our focus back to an external one, in order to essentially "come up for air". Introspection is done more effectively if we are willing to pace ourselves – take some time to think things through, let it go (go external), and come back (internal) and pick up where we left off if we have yet to resolve it. The more we stay internally-focused, the more we are forgetting to take the time to breathe.

Coming up for Air

So how does one go about making the switch from internal to external? Glad you asked.

Our senses are what connect us to the world outside of our mind. Sight, sound, taste, touch, and smell.

Sight. If it's a sunny day, get out and take in the beautiful light and colors. Watch a visually interesting movie or a sports game.

Sound. Put on some of your favorite music. Have an engaging conversation with a best friend.

Taste. Go to your favorite restaurant, or try a new one. Go to the supermarket and pick up some of your favorite foods. Cook yourself something amazing.

Touch. Get a massage. Learn how to do something craftsy with your hands. Cuddle with your partner.

Smell. Buy some scented candles or oils that have relaxing aromas, such as lavender. (Yeah, I'm a guy and I still said that.) Smell overlaps with taste, so that good tasting food will often smell great too. It can also overlap with sight, so that sunny day going for a nice hike in the woods will also often have relaxing scents atttached – the smell of fresh cut grass, blossoming trees and flowers.

When I am trying to get out of my head because it's become too busy or dark in there, I usually will consciously tell myself, "Stay on the surface", or "Come up for air". It becomes a personal mantra, reminding me to switch my focus.

◆　◆　◆

In the midst of a crisis it's very easy to become overly self-absorbed. It becomes all about our fears, our pain, our discomfort. And we lose focus on everyone else around us. We may feel alone in our pain, but we are also contributing to our own sense of isolation.

Part of coming up for air (going external) is reconnecting with the world around us, not just through one-sided activities, but staying involved (or getting involved) in the lives of others – hearing about their day, their struggles, their successes, continuing to maintain those relationships. Doing so gives our own mind a reprieve by stepping into someone else's world for a while and possibly restoring some balance to our perspective, remembering that we're not the only one who has stuff to deal with. There's always someone who has it worse than we do.

In becoming self-focused we can gravitate towards becoming just takers, and forget to give back. We may not feel like we have anything to give during those times, but we are missing the point that even just attempting to give/interact can help balance our focus, keep us on the surface, and do something meaningful at the same time.

Getting it Out

Part of fostering an external focus has to do with not just learning how to stay on the surface, but how we learn to get that inner stuff out. At some point a hoarder needs to purge the junk that they've been collecting, and we need to do the same with the junk we've been accumulating in our own heads.

Getting it out is usually done through self-expression. And self-expression is usually done through either speaking it or writing it.

Primal scream therapy, something done back in the late 1900's, involved shouting/yelling/screaming at the top of your lungs (preferably somewhere isolated or sound-insulated). The action would help get all of the internal emotion out until you'd exhausted yourself. While, by itself, it didn't solve underlying problems, it was one successful way to purge.

Similar to the primal scream, some will burn off anxious energy through pushing themselves with exercise. It's not being openly expressive, but it's still an external activity that helps quiet the brain.

Men, stereotypically, tend to internalize their emotions, not openly giving voice to what they're feeling. They might be able to talk about their feelings, but often struggle with being able to bring the actual emotion to the surface if it's anything other than anger. The vulnerability of it can be too uncomfortable for them. As with acknowledging need, they will often see it as showing weakness rather than strength, but fail to understand that it definitely takes strength to be vulnerable.

Women are typically given more permission at an early age to express themselves emotionally, moreso than men. Their ability to cry when they need to is a valuable skill. It's been said that with deep, heartfelt crying the body releases a particular chemical in tears that has a powerful healing agent.

Getting it out doesn't have to mean through showing the emotion, if forcing the emotion stops the process of getting it out. Just talking to a partner or friend, voicing what's going on – naming the fears, concerns and worries – is purging. *Sometimes just expressing what we're feeling allows the feeling to subside.* It just needed to be verbally acknowledged. That is one of the big reasons that talk therapy, just by itself, can still be effective.

One of the additional benefits of sharing our thoughts is that, if the conversation is interactive, then we are getting to go beyond our own perspective and getting to hear someone else's. The better we are at choosing who we share with, the better the feedback and insight we will get in return.

When it comes to communication, self-expression often creates an impasse that occurs between men and women. Men tend to be problem-solvers and women want to process. A woman may just want to voice what she's feeling, just to be heard and understood in order to be able to let it go, but the man may attempt to solve it for her – which wasn't what she was looking for. The man will fail to understand that just expressing oneself can be a solution of its own.

◆　◆　◆

When it comes to writing as a form of "getting it out", journaling is the typical method used to capture one's thoughts and feelings. Slightly different than the benefit of sharing our thoughts, the act of organizing them well enough to write them down actually helps our brain process what's going on in a way that we can't do just by juggling the thoughts in our head.

Sometimes, with journaling, if we keep a long enough record of our past experiences, we can begin to see our own problematic patterns as we've gone through life. Recognizing those patterns makes us more conscious of the circles we can get stuck in, what we have done during those times that either helped or hindered, and hopefully helps us to not repeat them so often.

Digestible Pieces

When we feel overwhelmed, often we are looking at a problem in its entirety and all of the possible complications that go along with it. But what makes it manageable is not trying to take on *all* of the problem at once. Instead, we're trying to look at just the next step or two in front of us, keeping it simple.

When I have a client do the priority exercise where they are assessing their life for overall balance, at the point they start strategizing how they are going to restore focus to the areas that are getting neglected, initially the plan is just looking at doable steps for the coming week. Baby steps. Things small enough that they can be done today or tomorrow. One step at a time. Restoring control and a more workable focus.

Big Picture/Little Picture

I mentioned this in my book on marriage, that when we're caught up in our problems of the moment we tend to get lost in the little picture we've created for ourselves, unable to see beyond our limited perspective. In those situations, ideally we're trying to shift our focus to the big picture perspective that also takes into account perspectives other than our own. Doing so allows us to see *beyond* our immediate self, opening us up to other solutions that we couldn't think of while stuck in our restricted vision. Sometimes this is accomplished by asking ourselves, "If it was my best friend struggling with this, what would I tell them to do?" I suggest this because often we have a better perspective when looking at the problems of others, rather than ourselves.

When a person is anxious or depressed, the walls of their world become very narrow. How they feel in that moment becomes everything, and part of their discomfort is with not knowing how long that moment will last. They assume that their little picture is actually the big picture, believing a distortion rather than recognizing that this is just one moment in time.

That's also why one's distress is usually felt more intensely at night. Because of the limited light, our awareness of the real world around us is restricted, our perspective easily becoming more distorted to whatever we project onto the darkness. Come daytime, when the sun's out, ideally we can leave our house and see the broader world around us, our fears scaling back down in size. Perspective has been expanded back to something that is closer to reality.

◆ ◆ ◆

Focusing on the big picture, however, is not always the best choice.

Not to overcomplicate this, but *the most healthy of us have learned to expand or contract our picture to whatever's best for the situation that we're currently in.* The "best fit" is whichever picture contains the most powerful positive for that situation.

If we are having a panic moment when we are going over a very tall bridge, setting off our fear of heights, we may need to shift to a bigger picture perspective that it won't be long until we've made it to the other side.

Or, if we're suffering from an injury or chronic health condition that has no end in sight, we may need to foster a small-picture perspective that just focuses on getting through the current day.

One of the visuals I think of for the little picture comes from the movie "Shrek", in which the donkey and the ogre are on the rope bridge with the fire and lava all around them. The donkey is paralyzed because he's taking too much in (big picture), but the ogre steps in and gets him to focus just on him (little picture). In removing the donkey's focus from the surrounding threat, he actually gets the donkey safely across to the other side.

So, a negative small picture means we reach for a positive big picture. Or, if we have a negative big picture, we go for a positive small one.

Reframing

The word "reframing" is used a lot in counseling, and fits nicely here since we're talking about pictures. Reframing is a third option that doesn't require us to go from big to little picture, or from little to big. Instead, it's basically taking the current picture, whatever size it is, and looking at it from a different angle, ideally restoring a degree of freedom and choice, or, at the least, finding a positive perspective to the same view. It's not lying to yourself, trying to trick your brain into thinking something's good when it's not. The practice simply acknowledges that there are often other, better perspectives than the ones we most easily gravitate to (the ones that make us feel the worst).

For instance, a person's been hanging on to a dead-end job far longer than they should have because it still gave them some small degree of security, and they fear change. But now layoffs are coming and they know it's only a matter of time before they're without work. They can either view it as a looming crisis that overwhelms them with anxiety to think about, or they can reframe it as an opportunity to finally move on and find something better.

Reframing can be difficult in that sometimes we're too close to our situation to see it any other way. In which case, we need others to help us find a better, more workable perspective. Sometimes that means a professional, but sometimes it simply requires a wise friend or partner.

Bullet Points:

- **An internal focus helps us with introspection and strategizing. An external focus helps us reconnect with the world around us and to participate in life. For balance, we need to be able to do both.**

- **Going from an internal focus to an external focus is accomplished by attending to our five senses.**

- **Sometimes we can purge our inner discomfort by getting our thoughts and feelings out through conversation or journaling.**

- **When a problem is too big, we need to break it down into digestible chunks, to just what our next one or two steps are going to be.**

- **Focusing on the positive big picture helps us see beyond our immediate negatives.**

- **The little positive picture helps us deal with surviving the problems that are too big to deal with in the current day, are chronic, or continuous – restoring focus to the present moment.**

- **Reframing changes the angle that we're viewing either the big picture or little one, to allow for a more positive interpretation that helps us shift our perspective and attitude in a better direction.**

Discussion Questions:

1. Do you tend to have more of an internal or external focus? Do you see an advantage to either? Are you able to shift between the two, or do you stay predominantly with just one? What do you, or could you, do to successfully make that shift when needed?

2. Are you able to get your emotions and thoughts out to those you're close to when needed? If not, what's standing in your way? What would make it easier to do? Do you understand that it's more of a skill than a personality thing? (In other words, anyone can get better at it.) Do you see the benefit of being able to do so? Have you ever attempted to get those emotions and thoughts out through writing them down?

3. Have you ever tried breaking a bigger problem down into doable steps?

4. Do you tend to be more of a big picture or small picture person? Are you able to shift between the two? What helps make that easier for you to do?

5. How is reframing different than shifting from big-picture to little-picture? Can you think of any negative thoughts or experiences you may have had, and then what reframing them would look like now that you can look back at them? Can you then apply the same technique to any current thoughts or events?

Chapter 6
Distraction

Many of the strategies for dealing with personal crises are focused on distraction – getting our mind off of it. And while this seems like a common sense solution, it really depends.

As I've already noted, we do need to take the time to consider what healthy emotional discomfort is trying to get us to pay attention to, because many times it's something that needs to be either acknowledged or fixed. If we keep disregarding or repressing it just because it feels uncomfortable then the underlying problem is going unsolved.

Let's say, though, that something has happened that we can't really change, and we have spent enough time taking the cause of our discomfort into account, so now we really need to move on to other things. When we are looking for distractions, there are two things we should be considering: 1) how strong is the distraction, and 2) how healthy is it?

How Strong?

Distractions will often work because our brain can only fully focus on one thing at a time (the key word being *fully*). The more I have something else center stage in my brain, the more the painful thought will, in that moment, lose its strength because it's now in the background and I am no longer feeding it. If I maintain that focus on something else, my brain will ultimately switch tracks and let the thought go, at least for a while. But I no longer have to stress over "what if it comes back" because I now have a powerful tool for dealing with it if it does.

Many will gravitate to using key phrases, positive mantras, that are powerful redirects for themselves. I've already mentioned some of the ones that I use, such as "stay on the surface", "come up for air", "one day at a time", and I will mention others as we go. Forgetting their symbolic power, just the repetition alone can be successful in leaving no room for the negative thoughts to be heard. Giving no time for the thoughts, the feelings that they create subside as well.

Part of the key with positive mental redirects is choosing ones that are significant for us on an individual level. If I just tell myself a cliche that my friend likes, while it may have sounded good, if it doesn't really resonate with me, then it is not going to be as successful.

Also, our personal mantras will shift in their effectiveness from day to day, which is why we need more than one. Just because one doesn't work as well in the moment as much as it did the day before, doesn't mean that it's lost its potency. It just means that, for that day, it wasn't as useful. Save it for another day.

◆　◆　◆

When it comes to choosing activities that redirect our brain, while we are also trying to choose positive activities that resonate with us (just like the positive mantras), we need to be choosing activities that require the majority of our focus to do. Just because I like to exercise, many types of exercise I can do without really having to focus. My body is performing the chosen task, but my brain is elsewhere. So now I will likely still have to use my mental redirects while I am exercising, which can be too much work.

Things like yoga, or martial arts, require so much attention to what we are doing in the moment in order to do it right that we don't have to be using mental redirects – the activity itself will be enough to occupy our mind.

We are also trying to choose activities that are directly connected to us taking care of us in meaningful ways, not just choosing empty time fillers. And, ideally, we have options that we consider to be our own particular personal passions. If we have no such passions, that can be a new, positive pursuit.

♦ ♦ ♦

Some crises occur just because there are a lack of current positives. We are all familiar with how a child, if denied positive attention, will seek it out in negative ways. In similar fashion, for some people, the most painful thing you can do is give them nothing to do, because they can't handle boredom. They require stimulation, and if they don't get it, they will typically act out in order to create some.

There are adults, some of whom have adult ADHD, who will create a crisis in their personal lives just because they need the stimulation that comes out of the resulting drama. They will usually not be conscious of what they are doing, but others around them can usually spot the chaotic pattern. Underneath it is a legitimate need for stimulation; they're just going about it in an unhealthy way.

When I was a kid, my parents attended a Presbyterian church that had an elderly pastor who, while well-intended, did not do well at capturing my attention with his somewhat monotone messages. I had to rely on my own imagination, and sometimes something to draw on (I liked to doodle), to get myself through the services. At one point, I started to tell myself shocking things to occupy myself, such as "What if you stood up and screamed at the top of your lungs right now in the middle of this quiet service?" I'd intentionally try to scare myself by thinking that I was just about to do it. That shiver down the back you get when you think of fingernails on chalkboard? I liked to see if I could make that happen.

But you have to be careful what patterns you start for your brain because, for some reason, mine decided to keep that shocking monologue going even outside of church. "What if you jumped off of that ledge?" "What if that car's going to swerve into your lane?" "What if that old person has a heart attack right in front of you?" "What if that's the last time you see your mom and dad?" At first, it was all just in fun – shock value. But I started to realize as life went on that my brain was still throwing out those thoughts, unsolicited, and they were no longer fun. Now they were making me anxious. Now they were problematic. But I didn't know how to make them just stop.

Like a muscle, the brain requires healthy exercise. Often, we fail to recognize how we exercise it in unhealthy ways until we've created a new neural pathway that's taken on a life of its own. However, that doesn't mean that we are incapable of either learning to discipline the pathway we've created, or carve a better path to take.

In an earlier book of mine, I mentioned a study involving the human brain where "normal" brains were compared to the brains of prison inmates. Because there were some differences noted, at first it was hypothesized that a criminal was born with a criminal brain. However, later evidence supported that most of us start with essentially the same brain but that the brain changes in shape and structure as we age, depending on life circumstances, diet, and how we exercise it (see Daniel Amen's work). Moreso, even into later years the brain is still resilient enough that it can alter its structure in response to better habits.

But here's the bottom line to what I'm saying. *The brain requires stimulation. If you don't give it something positive to focus on, it's going to gravitate to something negatively stimulating in order to get its stimulation fix.*

During a personal crisis, if our unhealthy negative thoughts are the most stimulating things we have to occupy our brain, it's going to be harder to get our brain to refocus on something else. If I have other positively stimulating things/activities/relationships to focus on, my mind is going to be more willing to give up its negative fixation because it's still being fed.

If I'm lacking in positive alternatives, that becomes part of the initial work of taking back personal control. I need to either restore those positive things/activities/relationships to my life, or create some new ones, that will stimulate my brain in positive ways.

How Healthy?

Healthy distractions can help alleviate some of the distress that negative thoughts create, but sometimes those same healthy distractions can alleviate the pain enough that we end up losing our motivation to deal with any unresolved problems – so, now, the healthy distractions are becoming unhealthy. That relief may even convince us, for a time, that the problem is solved.

I will often have couples come in for couple's work who, after a few sessions, are feeling better so they drop out of counseling, thinking that they're fixed. But, if they have yet to really master better tools for their issues, their problems aren't really solved. They just experienced some initial relief by putting energy back into their relationship.

If I feel bad about my lack of physical self-care and am starting to see some health issues develop, the necessary discomfort that I would hopefully experience exists to motivate me to get off my butt and go to a gym. But, if I distract myself with other things (work, eating, shopping, socializing, overly committing), I am not really helping the problem get any better.

If I have health-related anxiety, exercise can be *both* a healthy distraction and a solution to the underlying anxiety I'm experiencing, since I'm directly doing something about what's causing it.

Too much work needs the distraction of play. Too much time thinking needs the relief of being able to just be in the moment. Healthy distractions help balance us.

Healthy distractions are often where we have our fun. Fun, balanced distractions are vital. They serve a purpose even if their immediate utility isn't always obvious. Not all healthy distractions, of course, are related to the need for fun but most of them provide a necessary relief from stress.

What can often decide whether a distraction is healthy or not often comes down to how often it's engaged in, in comparison to everything else.

At the point where a healthy distraction starts to interfere with keeping other healthy priorities balanced, it's now becoming unhealthy. That doesn't mean you have to give up that distraction completely; instead, see if it can first be moderated. If, over time, you find that it's too powerful to moderate, you have to accept that it may hold too much of a draw for you to be able to continue to keep it in your life.

For many people, what starts out as a healthy distraction can become a negative because it turns into a singular focus. What makes this so difficult to see is due to the positives that can be coming out of the chosen activity. Say someone gets involved with the local church. They're overjoyed that they've found a meaningful way of contributing to the community that fits their personality. But, over time, they start to take on too much. It may not even feel like too much to them, but now it's starting to take time away from their family, they no longer have time for exercise, etc. – so it's costing them in other ways.

The True Distraction

There is a bigger point I want to make, though, regarding distraction and how our lives get off track, especially as it relates to personal crises.

Let's say that our lives are in relative balance, we're going along from day to day earning a living, trying to maintain our relationships, and get our personal needs met. But then a stressful event of some sort occurs. It can be a negative life circumstance, an intrusive thought that won't go away, a problematic relationship, but it's strong enough to disrupt our normal way of doing things.

living life → stressful event

From there, what's likely to occur is any number of negative emotions: anxiety, depression, guilt, panic, despair. In this case, let's say it's mostly anxiety.

living life → stressful event → anxiety

So, now that we have these negative anxious thoughts and feelings, if we don't find a successful way to resolve them, we will lean towards ways to distract ourselves from continuing to overly focus on our anxiety.

living life → stressful event → anxiety → distracting ourselves from the discomfort

When this happens, part of our personal dilemma can be that we have already expended so much energy on the anxiety that we have little energy left to do anything else. We're emotionally and physically exhausted. But doing nothing, under these circumstances, is practicing helplessness over our anxiety.

What we often fail to recognize in these situations is that *the real distraction is the anxiety itself.* It is distracting us from where we first started, when we were, ideally, living our lives well.

So, there are two strategies that I'm suggesting. The first strategy is that, sometimes, it's not really about exerting *more* energy (distracting ourselves from the distraction that anxiety creates), but learning to do *less.* In other words, we need to relearn how to not even invest the time and energy used in taking the anxiety rabbit trail. We have to catch ourselves starting on that path, recognize the choice involved, and take a more productive path, saving that energy for something else. ("Do less," can be a good personal mantra.)

This is different than repression or suppression. I'm not talking about ignoring the warning signs that healthy anxiety is creating. I'm talking about when we've done the due diligence of thinking it through, taking whatever necessary action is required of us, and now being at a place where we need to let it go.

So, if you're not going to expend your energy in worry, you're going to need to either learn to consciously conserve it (let it go, self-soothe, relaxation exercises, mindfulness, yoga) or expend it in a more useful way. In this case, the second strategy that I'm suggesting is not having to find new distractions but rather refocus your energy on what you were doing

61

before, when you were living your life well. If it was a healthy life, then there should be several positive activities that you can re-engage in that provide the necessary positive refocus. If not, then part of the problem may likely be that your life before was already out of balance, so you may have to look at what living life well would mean for you and start taking steps towards having that life.

living life → stressful event → anxiety/distraction → refocus energy back to living life well

◆　◆　◆

Panic attacks have a similar distractive tendency. Something sets off a panic attack but our focus is not usually on what set it off. Instead, we focus on the anxiety-provoking experience of the attack itself. So, the panic attack mistakenly becomes the identified problem rather than what initiated it.

However, if the focus remains on addressing what set off the attack, then we have a much better chance at preventing another attack from occurring. If the focus remains on the attack itself, we are now being distracted from the true problem because the attack is merely a symptom, not the cause, of our anxiety.

The healthiest distractions 1) also help us solve our underlying issues, 2) aren't just time fillers, 3) resonate with both who we are and who we want to be, 4) provide necessary relief but don't create new problems, 5) help keep our life in balance, and 6) are done in moderation.

Bullet Points:

- **Healthy distractions help provide necessary relief from stress, as well as assisting us in maintaining balance.**

- Unhealthy distractions simply fill time, don't help solve underlying problems, and often move our lives further out of balance.

- Distractions work in dealing with negative thoughts and feelings because our minds can usually only *fully* focus on one thing at a time.

- How effective a healthy distraction is usually depends on how successfully the distraction holds our attention and how well it resonates with our particular personalities.

- Our brains require stimulation.

- Some people require more stimulation than others.

- If we don't give our brains something positive to focus on, they will gravitate to whatever negative exists that is stimulating.

- We need to have sufficiently positive things/thoughts/people/ activities in our lives that provide the right kind of stimulation to feed our brains. That way, when there are significant negatives to focus on, we still have positive alternatives that are just as powerful, if not moreso.

- The true distraction in dealing with unhealthy negative thoughts are the thoughts themselves. They're distracting us from what we would be doing if we were living our lives well. Restoring the focus back to living well again restores our control.

Discussion Questions:

1. What distractions do you have to occupy yourself when you're bored or stressed? Thinking in terms of this chapter, are any of those distractions not really healthy?

2. Do you have any personal mantras? Are they mantras that are meaningful for you, or just borrowed ones? If you don't have any, what would finding some that were a fit for you look like?

3. How good are your distractions in terms of requiring your full focus? How good are they in terms of getting your head back to a better place?

4. Do you have any current personal passions? Did you before and you just gave them up over time? If so, would they still fit into your life in the present? If you have a partner, do you have any shared personal passions that help keep you connected?

5. What positively stimulating things/activities/relationships do you have in your life that effectively counter any negatives? Do you remember to turn to them when the negatives are threatening to steal your attention? If lacking in them, what do you need to do in order to bring some into your life?

6. Are you able to keep your distractions balanced, or do they move you to losing balance? Is moderation possible, and, if so, what does moderation look like? Do your distractions help you feel like you're taking better care of yourself, or lead you to feeling guilty over wasting important time?

7. Do you understand that the true distraction during times of personal crisis is how negative thoughts and emotions can move you away from living your life well? What would you be doing differently if you were back to living life well? How much of that can you still make happen now, despite the thoughts and feelings that might stand in your way?

Chapter 7
This Too Shall Pass

When we're in the middle of a personal crisis, sometimes we can't see any end to it, or at least a reprieve coming any time soon. In fact, part of what might be contributing to our pain is wondering if it will ever end – if our lives will ever go back to normal.

While it's true that crises can change us, challenge our thinking and emotional control, force us to reassess how we've been living our lives, it's also true that many crises are just passing storms. When we're in the middle of them, we can't see how long they're going to take to pass, but they still usually do. If we are able to view them as just one point in the middle of a progressive timeline, it can be easier to weather getting through them.

In line with this, I would add two new mantras – "This, too, shall pass," and "Ride it out."

For those who suffer from panic attacks, aside from the fear of the initial panic that initiates the "attack", there can also be a fear of remaining in that panicked state. But the reality is that that heightened state of arousal, at most, lasts up to 15 to 20 minutes before the body automatically cycles back down. For those who say their panic lasts longer, it's more likely that their continued anxious thoughts set off another cycle.

If we're looking at our periods of emotional distress as passing cycles, then part of getting through them is nurturing the attitude of riding them out. Just recognizing them as temporary and passing can give us a more removed emotional perspective that keeps us from getting swept up in them. We're now taking a step back, viewing the emotional flood as passing emotions and only problematic if we start treating them as the only reality.

Staying with panic attacks for a moment longer, many who have them develop this fear of re-experiencing what they felt the first time they had one. That first time it was completely unexpected, they didn't know what was going on, and this was a big contributor to why it escalated the way it did. But *the reality is that you can never go back to "square one"*. Meaning, you will never be in a position again where you are as unprepared, as vulnerable, as you were the first time. Each time it happens, you are gaining experience about what sets it off, that it does pass, and that there are things you do that makes it either better or worse.

But you need to be looking at your experiences critically, learning from them, in order to make the next time (if there ever is a next time) an easier process. The more we come to see extreme emotions as always being a distortion, not reality, just a passing wave, the less power they have over us. Each thing you learn from it gives you greater competency over handling it.

Crises and Time

At the age of about 10 years old I started to collect comic books. At first, reading comics was just an escape from boredom while at my grandmother's house in the country, where the TV had only three black-and-white channels with poor reception. Later, I became more interested in comics for the art. (For the professional, comics are referred to as "sequential art".) I learned to draw from copying what I saw, later taking a minor in art when I went to college and doing quite well at it. Of course, nowadays, comics are no longer viewed as a childhood nerdish hobby but promoted by mainstream culture as cool.

(Hang in there, I'm going somewhere with this.)

In the 80's, Frank Miller reinvented the Marvel comic character Daredevil, both through the type of story he told as well as his unique drawing style. (More recently, Daredevil has been given a wider audience through Netflix's Daredevil TV series.) For those who aren't familiar with the character, Daredevil was a normal human who went through a freak accident that took his sight but enhanced his other senses. In costume, however, everyone thinks the hero has sight because he's such an amazing fighter.

At one point in Miller's storyline, Daredevil's heightened senses go out of control and he becomes paralyzed with sensory overload. His old mentor, Stick, shows up and teaches him how to dim it down, getting it back under control.

This is what I think of when people go into crisis; that they have gone into sensory overload and everything has become magnified. The littlest thing is now experienced as a big thing. They can't trust their own senses and feelings, and, if they can't trust themselves (their own body and mind) then what can they trust? The one thing over which they felt they had some degree of control (their own life) is now in question.

But, as we learn how to deescalate ourselves, even in the midst of a crisis, with repeated successes we incrementally regain our sense of security and self-confidence. In the process, many of us will also have to come to terms with any illusions we may have harbored regarding just how much control we actually have over our lives. (Meaning, none of us have complete control.)

With situational crises, self-control usually comes back naturally, as the crisis passes, *even if we didn't do a good job of helping it pass.*

How big the crisis was will often predict the length of the recovery period, but even then a lot of that depends on personal resiliency. Some people snap back quicker than others. And some people actually do well in a crisis.

◆　◆　◆

The MMPI (Minnesota Multiphasic Personality Inventory) was more well-known in the 80's but is still used today in a revised format. While a personality measure, it is also used to make diagnoses and assess for thought disorders.

Everyone who takes the lengthy questionnaire ends up with a personal profile that has 10 clinical categories (such as Depression, Hypomania, Paranoia, etc.). Scoring below the level of significance in each category means that you have a profile that falls within the normal range of scores. Scoring *above* the level of significance for a category means that you're potentially diagnosable for that category. Everyone's profile usually has at least one or two "peak" scores – scores that are higher in one or two categories compared to the remaining scores, which indicate one's areas of vulnerability.

One of the interesting things about the MMPI is that, once you know what a person's peak scores are, you can pretty accurately predict what their issues are going to be if they go into crisis. What you will often see is that, even if they tested normal, in crisis their peak scores will now elevate, sometimes above the level of significance. So the issues that they normally manage, in crisis, now start to manage them.

The good news is that, once the crisis has passed, their level of functioning (and their profile scores), predictably, will return to normal.

When there is No Going Back to Normal

Even in the extreme situations, when the crisis is dealing with something that has made a permanent change in your life, when there is no going back to "normal" (such as the death of a loved one, the war veteran who has lost a limb, or the parents who lose a child), even in these situations, *there is still a progression.*

It would be easy to view these scenarios as storms that will never pass, but the storm itself was having to go through the initial loss – what the survivor is now having to deal with is the storm's aftermath. They still live. They survived. But it's not the life that they were used to, or the life that they wanted. However, if at some point they decide to do more than just survive – to choose life again – they start learning to adjust, to cope, to compensate, and to adapt. It may require reinventing themselves or their life to a degree, but, gradually, they are creating a new kind of normal. They will still carry the scars with them from what happened, but life will go on.

Often, *how well someone is able to weather storms of that magnitude has to do with how open or resistant they are to accepting change.*

Many of you are probably familiar with Kubler-Ross's 5 stages of grief: denial, anger, bargaining, depression and acceptance. While the model is focused on the grief over losing a loved one, it is easily generalized to any significant loss or crisis. While they are stages, they aren't necessarily sequential. So, when you're going through a loss, you may tend to bounce back and forth between the stages. You need to give yourself permission to go through them at your own pace, but try not to rush the process or you might skip a necessary step to truly get to acceptance.

Even at the point of acceptance, you can still get pulled back into the grief cycle and have to do some work to get back to acceptance once again. But, if you got there once, it's easier to walk that same path again, because now you know the way.

Acceptance is getting to, "It happened. I can't change it. Life goes on. While I mourn the loss of what was, I am still grateful for what I had before that, and trying to find new appreciation for what I still have left. Is there anything I need to learn from what happened? How am I going to make the most of the life that remains in front of me?"

◆　◆　◆

At the risk of minimizing significant loss (which I don't want to do), there's one final story from the comic world that I feel the need to share.

I, like C.S. Lewis, love Celtic and Norse mythology. Back in the mid-80's Walt Simonson did a historic run on the comic "Thor", most notably bringing some of the actual Norse mythology into the book. As most people know from the Marvel movies, Thor, the god of thunder, was the son of Odin, the All-father.

In Simonson's telling, Odin, after an epic battle with Surtur, the king of fire demons, is supposedly killed, and Thor, in his grief, wanders off into the wilderness and gets caught in an avalanche. He wakes up in an ice cave, injured, where an old man is helping him recuperate.

The old man has an unusual hobby of carving miniature ice sculptures of people that, when he breathes on them, come to life. However, being made of ice, they only live for a day and then melt by the fire at night.

Thor becomes fascinated with them because they can speak, are self-aware, and, while they live, they dance. He has a hard time understanding why they celebrate if they know they only have a short time before they're going to reach their end, but they make the point that that's why they dance – they want to make the most of the time that they have, so that there are no regrets.

I would say the same thing – *the only thing we truly have to fear in this life is not making the most of the time that we have.* Not that you should dance your life away, because life as a constant party could easily become wasting your life, but that we each need to look at life (any life) as precious, and our time as valuable. We need to take the time to stop and smell the roses, rather than getting lost in only obligation, achievement and responsibility. We need to make intentional choices about how we're spending our time, and who we're spending it with, attaching a priority to quality over quantity, and meaningful over meaningless.

Emotional Wounds vs. Trauma

When a person remains in crisis, even though the crisis has passed, it raises the question of whether the associated distress is trauma-related.

Trauma-related emotional pain is connected to a past traumatic event that leaves us essentially stuck in time. It could be something that happened as a child, or it could have happened later in our lives. But because we can't go back and do things differently, we don't know how to resolve it in the present.

We may not even recognize that we've become stuck, but when new events occur in our lives we respond in a way that's not in perspective to that present moment, because emotionally it's now being connected to that past event.

Not to make this overly complicated, but there is a difference between a trauma and an emotional wound. An emotional wound will usually heal over time if we stop picking at it, whereas a true trauma is more resistant to healing itself. Also, an emotional wound tends to be more restricted to just the wounded area, whereas a trauma tends to have a more global impact on almost every other area of one's life. For example, someone with an emotional wound from a bad romantic relationship now has trust issues with future romantic relationships. However, the trauma victim may have difficulty in numerous settings – their relationships, their work, and their personal life – all due to that one traumatic experience.

If that trauma goes back to childhood, the problem is additionally complicated because the trauma occurred at a point before their brain had fully developed.

The neo-cortex ("new brain") is the last part of our brain to mature. It is the area of our brain that involves higher-reasoning processes and doesn't fully develop until somewhere between the ages of 17 and 24. If a trauma occurred prior to the brain being fully formed it is likely that the experience of that event never got fully processed at that age, because the brain still didn't have the capability to do so. So the emotional experience of that event still resides in the primitive brain, disconnected from the rational part necessary to put it all into perspective. It becomes "unfinished business".

As a result, when an event (or our own thinking) in the present agitates that memory, we respond very primitively, often with the emotions and reactivity of the child that experienced them way back when. There is often a hypervigilance, or oversensitivity, with the traumatized because the wound has never healed and anything that comes close to it can set it off.

71

For the traumatized population, to learn to move past the trauma usually requires getting help, since their brain is having difficulty adjusting on its own. The good news for them is that help is available. One of the most promising interventions today for dealing with traumatic histories is something called Eye Movement Desensitization and Reprocessing (EMDR), developed by Francine Shapiro. Initially, it had a lot of success with war veterans, but nowadays it's used with a variety of different traumas with continuing positive results.

If I can roughly summarize how EMDR works, the brain of the traumatized individual has a frozen memory, the emotional piece remaining unresolved. So, now, when they have another experience that has a similar theme or emotion, it becomes attached to that older unresolved memory, like building a row of dominos. New negative connections keep knocking over the domino chain, each time setting off an overreaction. The present and the past keep overlapping. EMDR, by reprocessing the memories, separates the emotional connection between those different memories, so now each of those events no longer overlaps. As a result, the traumatized individual no longer has the cumulative emotion in the present built up from their past memory, so present events remain in perspective.

◆ ◆ ◆

There was an interesting study done a while ago on a "normal" population versus a traumatized one. Both groups were shown a movie where there were shocking subliminals inserted every so often, appearing too quickly to register consciously but long enough for the unconscious brain to notice. The "normal" group's brainwaves registered a startle response the first time a subliminal appeared, and then the next, and the next. But as time went on, they reacted less and less, adjusting to the shock. The traumatized group also had a similar startle response, but the difference was that their brains never acclimated to the subliminals. They continued to react each time.

As far as "this, too, shall pass", that study made the point that the brain has a natural adaptability that adjusts over time to stressors – *even if the stressors themselves remain present, and even if we're not consciously doing anything to make them better.* That's not an excuse for you to do nothing if you're in a position where you can do something to improve things, but it's saying that even if you are in a position where you can't do anything, your brain can still make positive adjustments of its own given the time to adapt.

Bullet Points:

- **Negative emotional waves will naturally pass with time if we let them.**

- **So long as we are learning from our experiences, we learn competency over dealing with them.**

- **Comic books are cool.**

- **During times of crisis, the things we normally manage will predictably become more difficult to manage. As the crisis passes, our issues will typically go back to manageable.**

- **Just being aware of what happens to us during crisis (our predictable patterns) can make it easier to move through a crisis.**

- **With trauma-related anxiety, our brain becomes stuck in time, experiencing in the present the intensity of something that happened in the past. This is especially true for things that occurred to us as children, before our brains could work through and resolve what happened to us.**

- **Trauma-related anxiety usually requires getting help. EMDR is one of the most effective modern interventions for helping to get relief from it.**

- **Even if a problematic situation doesn't go away, our brain naturally learns to better adapt to the stress of it. In addition to what our brain does naturally, learning useful tools makes the process that much easier.**

Discussion Questions:

1. If you've experienced crises before, did things go back to normal when they passed? Did you do anything in particular to help the crisis pass? Did you feel more competent for having gotten through it? What about other people you've seen go through crisis? How did they get through it? Did they get back to normal or was it a different kind of normal?

2. When it comes to emotional waves, are you able to ride out your own waves or do they tend to knock you over every time? What do you do that makes it easier to ride out your own wave? What about other people's emotional waves – are you able to tolerate other people's pain, knowing it may just be a wave, even if it's directed at you?

3. Does the knowledge that "with situational crises your internal world typically goes back to normal once the crisis has past" help ease any of your own concerns? What about the knowledge that, even when a crisis creates permanent changes, a healthy progression back to living life is still possible?

4. What is the difference between an emotional wound versus a trauma? How would you classify your own emotional injuries? If you've ever had an emotional wound, how did it heal – did it heal over time on its own, did you do something to help it heal, or did others help make it better? If you've ever suffered a trauma, how did you get past it? If you haven't gotten past it, are you willing to get help for it?

Chapter 8
Mindfulness – Body & Mind

There are four broad areas in our lives that we need to work at keeping healthy because they will help keep us resistant to crisis: body, mind, heart and spirit. While the categories may be broad, the tools for each are very specific. I will be covering them over these last three chapters. I like to think of the categories as "the four elements", because they parallel the four elements found in nature.

When it comes to the first two elements, body and mind, they are interrelated when it comes to understanding *mindfulness*.

When I first started practicing counseling in the 80's, the term "mindfulness", for the most part, simply referred to being self-aware – aware of our self-talk, our current feelings, and the feedback that our body gives us as to its current state of tension or relaxation. It was about knowing how to be present in the moment, rather than lost in the past or way off in a projected future.

When I was doing focused couple's work some years later, practicing mindfulness meant helping each partner to be more aware of the words they were using with each other and choosing better ones, watching the body language that each was unconsciously projecting, recognizing the unhealthy patterns that the couple would get caught up in, and the level of their own reactivity – doing a better job of not just self-soothing, but soothing each other. Mindfulness was expanded beyond self-awareness to now include other-awareness.

Today, mindfulness is a movement of its own, and sometimes a stand-alone therapy. When it comes to moving through crisis, or preventing it, practicing mindfulness is vital. If we aren't aware of our self-talk (what we tell ourselves that gets us so upset), then we can't correct it or redirect it. If we aren't in touch with our initial physical agitation that is the predictable precursor to escalating panic or feeling overwhelmed, then we often miss our early opportunities to do our own self-intervention at a point where our inner state is still manageable. If we can't see the things that we do that makes things worse, then we won't know what to do to make them better.

The Earth Element

Body, the first element, is the *physical* aspect of our health, and is similar to the element of earth. Earth is often thought to be the strongest of nature's elements, yet it can be eroded away by any of the other elements. So, too, our physical health, the most visible aspect of health for us to be able to focus on, can be positively or negatively impacted by any of the other three aspects/elements.

While I mentioned in Chapter 1 that emotional issues can sometimes be caused by a physical condition, there are also times when a physical condition can be created because of our emotional distress. When we are not willing to address our own stress, our body will still communicate to us that it's feeling it by developing physical symptoms (headaches, ulcers, high blood pressure, muscle pain, arthritis, etc.).

Many inflammatory diseases are thought to be either created or exacerbated by emotional suppression. If we typically repress our negative emotions rather than let them out (expressing them in healthy ways), there is often a greater cost of what it does to us from the inside out.

Typically, when we find better ways of addressing and expressing those emotions, the associated physical conditions get better. Thinking proactively, if we keep our bodies in good health, then our immune systems remain strong, and our resistance to stress is greater. When in crisis, *regular exercise becomes of vital importance in getting through it.* While there is the obvious physical benefit, exercise also strengthens us both mentally and emotionally.

◆　◆　◆

Sleep is often an overlooked factor with our physical health, but it plays a major role in either how quickly someone deteriorates in a crisis, or actually leads to a crisis occurring. A good night's rest helps recharge us and keep our faculties clear. Some of us require more than 8 hours and some of us require less, but lack of sleep saps our energy, distorts our perception, and weakens our resistance to stress. The complication, of course, is that while a chronic lack of sleep can lead us more quickly into crisis, crisis itself makes it harder to sleep.

When we have difficulty with sleep often tells us something about the underlying issues that are affecting our sleep. Difficulty getting to sleep usually indicates that someone is struggling with anxiety. Chronic middle of the night awakenings usually indicates a medical problem (most often undiagnosed reflux). Early morning awakenings, with a failure to return to sleep, is typical of depression.

Sleep hygiene is all about the environmental factors and routines that contribute to, or interfere with, getting a good night's rest. Here are a few of the hygiene guidelines:

1) Go to bed at the same time each night.

2) Set the temperature of your bedroom to a comfortable degree.

3) Buy a good supportive mattress, one that doesn't retain too much heat.

4) Don't go to bed hungry – a light snack before bedtime is allowable so long as it's not greasy or heavy food.

5) If you have reflux/GERD, disregard #4. Don't eat anything 3 hours prior to bedtime. Sleep with your upper body elevated, but

not so that you are bent at the waist (which puts undue pressure on your stomach).

6) Fewer liquids before bedtime means fewer sleep interruptions to use the bathroom. Restrict caffeine and alcohol. (Many people will use alcohol to get to sleep but it actually creates late night awakenings.)

7) Plan for the next day earlier in your evening so your brain isn't occupied with this when you go to bed.

8) Don't try to force yourself to fall asleep. The more you force it, the harder it will be for it to happen – your brain already knows how to do it, you just have to get out of the way and let it.

9) Turn your clock away so you can't see it. People who watch the clock have more sleep interruptions.

10) Avoid napping. Napping will reduce your sleep demand at night, effecting your sleep length and quality.

11) Make your bedroom comfortable but free from light and random noise.

12) Do not put a TV or computer, anything stimulating, in your bedroom.

13) Regular exercise makes it easier for your body to sleep since it burns off anxious energy. While it's not a good idea to exercise just before bedtime, since expending energy creates energy, there are different opinions as to how close to bedtime it should be. The practice of yoga, because it relaxes both the body and mind, would be something you could do closer to bedtime than something that was more stimulating.

14) Use any of the scents (such as lavender) and oils that promote sleep and relaxation.

15) Consider using any of the sleep apps available that use a combination of music, sounds or guided messages to aid falling asleep.

16) Sleep meds during a crisis can sometimes be a temporary necessity, but are otherwise something you should use sparingly and not be reliant on.

Relaxation and Breathing

Part of mindfulness is learning to self-regulate. In other words, if we notice we're physically tense, then we take steps to relax that tension. If we notice we're using harsh words, then we do a better job of editing what comes out of our mouths. If we can catch the stressful thoughts we're telling ourselves, then we change the self-talk.

One of the most immediate and basic steps to relaxing our minds and bodies is through our breathing. Breathing regulates our heart rate and blood pressure. It also determines how much oxygen we're taking in, which affects the oxygen supply to our muscles – making them tense or relaxed.

Breathing exercises serve multiple purposes. Aside from the physical impact they have on relaxation, they also serve as: 1) a distraction technique, since we are focusing on just our breathing, 2) a way of letting go of everything else in that moment, 3) a form of "doing less", conserving our energy, and 4) a way of training our brain to relax on demand.

I'm not going to go into detail about all of the various breathing techniques available to manage stress as you can simply google any number of them for yourself. I will mention just one, the 4-7-8 technique. Pressing the tip of your tongue to the roof of your mouth and keeping it there, you inhale through your nose for a slow count of 4, hold it for a count of 7 and exhale through your mouth to a count of 8. You do this repetition about 4 or five times, twice a day, as part of your daily routine, as well as during those times when you feel yourself starting to become stressed or anxious. Over time, it teaches your brain to relax when it receives this cue of 4-7-8.

◆　◆　◆

Yoga is one of the best forms of exercise. It progressively challenges you, the results tend to be relatively immediate, and it is an exercise routine that you can carry with you into old age. Because the forms that go with yoga can be complicated, they require your full focus, getting your mind off of everything else. And because yoga is centered on your breathing, you are also getting practice with breathing techniques. Further, yoga gives your brain practice at just being in the moment, narrowing your focus to just your breath and going through the forms. It's a very helpful way to carve a new neural pathway in your brain to focus and relax.

Men will tend to shy away from something like yoga, often thinking it's more for women, not aggressive enough, or something they'd be embarrassed to do in a class. But you can do yoga in the privacy of your own home with the simple use of a DVD to walk you through it. Some instructors will focus more on the meditative aspects to yoga, while others will focus on the physical forms, so be selective in what you're looking for.

The Water Element

Mind, the second element, encompasses the realm of our *thoughts*. Similar to water in its natural state, our thinking can be quite fluid and malleable, allowing us to be creative and adjust to new information. However, as with water turning into ice, our thinking can also become overly rigid and resistant to change.

Whether crises are situational or self-created, we have to look at the possible *thought distortions* that we engage in that contribute to creating or maintaining them, and replace them with healthier, more reality-based cognitions.

Thought distortions can be personal myths that we are buying into (for example, thinking that your partner should know what you need without having to say anything), a lack of education about the probabilities of something actually happening (such as the likelihood of a plane crash), or leaps of logic that are attached to personal fears we may possess (like thinking that nobody's trustworthy or reliable because you've been hurt before).

Here's some of the more typical thought distortions that can contribute to crises:

All-or-nothing thinking, or *black-and-white thinking,* is when the thinking is limited to two extremes. I'm either great or I'm a failure. If I can't do something well, then I don't want to do it at all. If I can't have it exactly the way I want, then I don't want it. There is only acceptance or rejection. It's either right, or it's wrong. It's good, or it's bad.

The obvious problem with this is that it's overly simplistic thinking and fails to recognize the complexity of many situations and issues. It tends to lean towards quick judgments rather than doing the work of considering the pros and cons, other perspectives, creative alternatives, compromise, or moderation.

It's an immediate conclusion of "You don't love me" in response to necessary, loving, criticism by another. Or, "That's the wrong way to do that", when there really is no wrong or right way, it just wasn't your way. It's a "He's not a good person", when he made one visibly poor choice.

Catastrophizing or **awfulizing** is when we make things worse than they are, gravitating to whatever the worst-case scenario might be. Small things are made into big things with little or no sense of perspective.

"This was the worst day ever!" Rather than, "Today was not a good day for me."

"He's the worst person on the planet!" Rather than, "I really didn't like what he did."

"This situation is hopeless!" Rather than, "This is really stressing me out."

"My life is over!" Rather than, "I'm feeling overwhelmed right now."

Along similar lines, **overgeneralization** is taking one or more events and generalizing them to an extreme. "Never" and "always" tend to get thrown into the mix.

"He does this all the time!" Rather than, "He does this often enough that it's bothering me."

"This is never going to change!" Rather than, "It's upsetting me that things have yet to change as much as I would like."

You may not see much of a distinction between the two statements, but one is more accurate and therefore more rooted in reality. The more we buy into the distortion, the more we are straying from the truth of what it is and what it isn't, often making the difference between feeling hopeless versus still open to finding solutions.

Mental filter is when we allow a single comment or event to drown out any other information that might conflict.

Frank: "That was a really great week we had."

Milly: "I can't believe you said that. It was a horrible week! Remember that fight we had?"

Frank: "Sure I do, but we talked it out and that was only one evening out of the whole week that didn't go so well."

Milly: "Well, for me, it ruined the whole week."

Magical thinking is when we mystify the meaning behind events in either a negative or positive direction – interpreting coincidences as fate, or a chance meeting as "meant to be".

"I'm doomed to fail."

"We're so blessed. Nothing bad is ever going to happen to us."

"This is God's way of punishing me for what I did."

"I don't care what anyone else says, I know that she's my soul mate."

The reality is that some things occur just due to coincidence. Some things happen simply due to cause and effect. Not everything has a deeper meaning.

When magical thinking becomes integrated into our spiritual lives, errors in thinking can be more difficult to discern because they can be fed by one's own faith. If that occurs, we can be at risk of overly spiritualizing our experiences to the degree that we're no longer living in the real world, and may even be contributing to our own crisis, depending on what we're concluding.

For instance, if I believe that everything is preordained (decided ahead of time by God), and therefore there is no free will, then I may take it to the extreme that I'm not really responsible for anything that I do because I was destined to do it. Or, I may have a hard time with the idea of a loving God because I see God as being responsible for not just the good, but every bad thing that happens.

Caution and discernment are important factors when attempting to look for deeper meaning with our experiences, but both tend to be harder to practice effectively when we're already in crisis.

Discounting the positive is minimizing the positive when it occurs, like those who can't take a compliment.

A few paragraphs back, when Milly told Frank that it was a horrible week, not only was that using a mental filter, it was also an example of both awfulizing and discounting the positive.

Someone does something quite thoughtful for another, but it's responded with thinking, "She didn't really mean that." Or, "That's not going to make up for what happened yesterday." Or, "If he really wanted to be thoughtful, he should have gotten me flowers instead."

When we're going through a crisis, we need to be actively focusing on as many potential positives as we can, appreciating what's still working, since, otherwise, crises push us towards a negative mindset that sees only what's wrong, or what could go wrong.

———————

Mindreading is when we automatically assume that we know what someone else is thinking without bothering to check it out.

"I know she doesn't like me."

"He thinks I'm a loser."

"She's just trying to use me."

While we all form our theories about how others think or feel, the problem becomes when we treat our theories as truth rather than practice the benefit of the doubt. In those situations, we typically won't attempt to get better information by asking directly, or talking to others. And, even if we do, we may still not trust the information we get.

People will sometimes use mindreading approaches as a backwards way to get information from someone. "I know you don't like me," can actually be an attempt to be assured that they *are* liked. However, this comes across as manipulation, which it is, even if it's not consciously intended that way.

———————

Fortune telling is when we automatically assume the worst about the future.

Someone talks themselves out of a relationship before they've even given it a chance. Or they don't apply for a job because they're predicting that there's no way that they would get it. And because they're predicting a particular negative outcome, they're either assuring, or at least increasing the likelihood that it will occur.

If I'm concluding "I'm going to screw up," chances are I will because I'm approaching it with that expectation.

Problematic relationships develop when either partner practices *helplessness* by routinely predicting what the other will do in response to what they do. As a result, they give up their positive behavior because they're convinced they know the other's response will be negative.

"If I dress up for him tonight, he's not even going to notice."

"If I share with her what happened with my day, she's just going to find something to judge about it."

Historically, these conclusions may be partially justified, but the problem is that now there is an absence of positive effort altogether.

"Should" statements are statements we tell ourselves (and others), that include the word "should", and indicate only one right way to do things. There are the shoulds that we are taught as children:

"You should say you're sorry if you've hurt someone."

"You should look both ways before you cross the road."

"You should eat everything that's on your plate."

"You should listen to what you're told."

"You should chew your food with your mouth closed."

"You should respect authority."

As we enter the dating years, we learn new "shoulds", which vary, based on who we talk to:

"A man should open a door for a woman."

"A woman should always speak well of her man."

"You should never cheat on your partner."

"You should save sex for when you're exclusive with someone."

"The man should initiate asking the woman out."

"A woman should offer to pay on the first date."

As adults, hopefully we have revised our list of "shoulds" to those that are the most necessary, healthy and functional.

"You should practice taking ownership for the things you do wrong."

"You should try to do your best at the things that matter the most."

"You should be honest."

"You should practice integrity."

"You should take other's thoughts, feelings and needs into account."

"You should try to live a balanced, intentional life."

But some of the "shoulds" that adults still practice can be taken too far, becoming overly nitpicky, getting stuck in sexist thinking, or being relationally dysfunctional.

"You should always clean your dishes immediately after you eat."

"The laundry should be done exactly like this."

"A man should never show weakness."

"The woman should submit to the man."

"Children should be seen but not heard."

"If you love me, then you should do what I say."

"To be happy in life, you should marry and have kids."

"If you are a success, then you should have a big home, a small fortune, and a beautiful partner."

While healthy "shoulds" set necessary limits for us, creating order and direction in our lives, unhealthy "shoulds" become oppressive, overly restrictive and often don't work in the real world. "Shoulds" can also become problematic when there are too many, making a rule for everything – so that either we, or everyone else in our lives, always end up falling short. Freedom and choice become lost when we are living in bondage to too many "shoulds".

Many personal crises are due to either too many "shoulds", or when we practice unhealthy "shoulds". Which is why, at different points in life, each of us needs to re-examine our "shoulds", deciding if they still make sense and work for us, or if they're a part of the problem.

For others, the problem is the opposite. They are *lacking* in "shoulds" and need to add some to their list if their life is going to function better, because without sufficient structure and limits, we risk living a chaotic, narcissistic life.

Personalization is when we give too much negative credit for something that was not entirely, or maybe not even remotely, about us.

For instance, a girl meets a guy at a social gathering. She likes him, but he doesn't seem to really be into her. She tortures herself the rest of the evening trying to figure out what's wrong with her that he wasn't interested. In truth, his lack of interest may have had little or nothing to do with her.

For another, a neutral, innocent comment or action is automatically interpreted as an intentional attack, something that was knowingly directed at hurting them.

Blame is when we fault other people or circumstances for a problem, overlooking our own contribution to the situation.

"I lost that job because they had it in for me from the start."

"My life would have gone so much better if I'd have had different parents."

"You ruined my whole day."

"I wouldn't have said those cruel things if you'd just have been nicer to me."

The person who fails to emotionally mature in life is the one who fails to learn to take responsibility for their own actions. Their relationships remain superficial because they can't really experience true intimacy if they are never able to take ownership for their part.

The bottom line is that nobody *makes* us do or feel anything. They may *influence* our behavior and emotions, but they don't ultimately decide those things for us, we do.

◆　◆　◆

It's not my intent to exhaustively cover thought distortions in this chapter, because correcting these kinds of issues is a book in itself. I did want you to be aware, though, of what they look like. I will spend some time in Chapter 9 talking about redirecting such distortions and negative thinking. If you find that you struggle with thought distortions, have been accused of recurring distortions, or just want to do some focused exploration, I would refer you to the works of David Burns ("Feeling Good", "Intimate Connections", "10 Days to Self-Esteem", and "When Panic Attacks").

Being too mindful

For the person who obsesses and overthinks, they may say that part of the problem is that they are already *too* mindful of what is going on with their body and in their head. So, the last thing they want to do is spend more time there.

Yet, for the overly mindful, healthy mindfulness isn't asking you to focus even more on the negative information that you are already torturing yourself with. If you've already done what you could to address the cause of your discomfort and now it's just dealing with excess worry, healthy mindfulness would help you to: 1) be more aware of when you're engaging in your negative patterns, 2) recognize the choice you have with what you focus on, 3) teach you how to shift your focus to a more peaceful place, 4) help you stay on the surface, doing less, and 5) narrow your attention to just being present and in the moment.

◆　◆　◆

At the end of my eighth grade school year, I developed a fear of public speaking after an experience I had in the annual school play. It all started with just one anxious thought I told myself a few days before the play was to occur. I was the lead male role and had many pages of lines I had to remember. Out of nowhere the thought popped into my head, "Why do you think you're going to be able to remember all of your lines, especially in front of a public audience?" Prior to that, the thought had never even occurred to me. But once I had that thought, since I had no prior experience to rely on that I would be successful, it made me physically sick, and I couldn't stop thinking about it until the play was over.

During the first act, due to my stress, I developed a dry, scratchy throat and couldn't stop intermittently coughing. Luckily, my character was supposed to be sick, but it was still noticeable. During intermission, I was given an ice cube to suck on, which fixed things so I was able to finish the second act just fine. But I was still left with feeling like I'd failed and not wanting to put myself in that position ever again.

As I got older, when I would see good speakers or actors, I would feel stressed just wondering what I'd be feeling if I were in their shoes. I admired that they were able to get past their own fears and do what they did so well.

At one point, I had a conversation with one such speaker and asked him how he was able to do it. He smiled and answered that those thoughts just didn't occur to him. He really didn't think about that stuff. He was just focused on saying what he needed to say. For some reason, I had never considered that. I had just assumed that everyone struggled with some degree of speech anxiety if they had to give a speech. So it was a surprise to realize that it wasn't this tremendous ability this guy had that I didn't, his mind just didn't go there. He wasn't doing more than me to manage his anxiety, he was actually doing a whole lot less, and was successful because of it. But, for me, once that particular anxious thought was there, it changed everything.

I was being *overly* mindful of my own thoughts and feelings. The only thing that speaker was mindful of were the words with which he was choosing to express himself.

Attitude of Gratitude

Good, sincere, self-probing questions increase our degree of mindfulness. "Why is that so upsetting for me?" "Why am I feeling this way?" "What am I feeling?" "What am I doing that's not working?" "What am I doing that works?" "What am I learning about myself by going through this?"

Part of that self-exploration is looking at our underlying attitudes toward life and the everyday. Have your recurring struggles made you bitter, resentful, or seeing only the negative? Has your overall attitude towards life become one of looking for (and dwelling on) the bad before the good? If true, people need to work at developing an "attitude of gratitude".

While there is always the negative, there is also always the positive. Which you choose to focus on is going to shape your perspective and ability to handle stress and times of crisis. Focusing only on the negative saps your energy and usually doesn't inspire change. It remains problem-obsessed.

I see couples who have long lists of how each has failed the other, yet ask them to identify their partner's strengths and what's still working, and they will struggle with being able to think of anything. It's not that those things no longer exist, it's just that the couple is now so overly focused on the negative that they no longer see, and give any recognition for, the good. Usually, if I press the couple, helping their minds make the shift, they can start to identify positives that are still present but are getting minimized, having fallen into their blind spots.

Balancing the negative with the positive keeps us more connected to reality, allows us to be more solution-focused, motivated, and open to new opportunities.

◆　◆　◆

When it comes to approaching change, in both relationships and with one's self, it's important to understand the difference between *conviction* versus *condemnation*.

91

If I condemn someone I'm in relationship with, I'm judging their *character* – rejecting them for who they are. ("You are useless." "You are so stupid." "You are a waste of space.") Who they are isn't likely to change, so rejecting them on that level isn't going to inspire change or allow much of a future for the relationship. In fact, using verbal judgments increases the likelihood that change is *not* going to occur.

Even if we are only saying those things in our head about the other person, we are paving the way to lose any remaining respect we may have for them, and it will be reflected in our outward behavior towards them.

By contrast, conviction focuses on confronting the problematic *choices* and identifying healthier choices – which is more likely to be doable. Because it's solution-focused, it's more motivating and supports necessary change. You can love someone and still not be okay with what they're choosing to do. While using conviction is still offering a criticism, it's a healthier path when attempting accountability.

For those with self-esteem issues, there is the tendency for them to hear *any* criticism (even a healthy, necessary one) as a rejection and, therefore, unloving. But they have to learn that in an adult, mature relationship, you hold each other accountable by providing such feedback because you love each other and you want the relationship to work and to grow. If you didn't provide necessary criticism you would actually be practicing neglect of the relationship.

I say all of this because, in times of crisis, the person going through the crisis is often using condemning self-talk with themselves rather than exercising self-conviction. Often, one of their inner voices is that of a *critical* parent talking to them in a condemning way versus a convicting way. And they probably never learned the difference between the two, such as with the man who internally beats himself up (calling himself "weak" or "a loser") whenever he's feeling vulnerable, anxious, stressed or depressed.

While they still need to hold themselves accountable if change is necessary, they need to adopt an inner *supportive* parent's voice. That voice is focused more on correcting any current problematic choices, rather than passing judgment on themselves for their role in creating or contributing to the current crisis.

People who practice condemnation tend to have a judging nature, gravitate more towards anger, and often have a lot of unreasonable expectations of others. Their attitude tends to naturally focus more on what's wrong than what's right. If so, it's time for an attitude shift.

When it comes to consciously developing an attitude of gratitude, our personal daily accountability involves intentionally identifying, and being grateful for, everything that is still working in our life. It's learning to focus on recognizing and giving credit for both our own and others' positive choices, giving and being able to receive compliments, and underlining our own personal positive qualities and strengths (as well as noting them in others).

◆　◆　◆

Maintaining a positive attitude is easier when you have positive things to look forward to. For someone with an internal locus of control, they don't wait for positive things to happen to them, they make them happen. They will consciously create oases for themselves (upcoming fun events, breaks and enjoyable routines) that leads to positive anticipation of what's ahead.

There was a study done many years ago interviewing elderly individuals in their 90's or above who self-reported as still enjoying life. The study was trying to see if there were any particular factors the elderly had in common that might have contributed to their longevity.

One factor they had in common was that they all had retained a sense of humor, not taking themselves, or life, too seriously. They attributed that humor to helping them keep things in perspective, adding a light to their lives when times were dark.

A second factor was that they all had things that they still looked forward to, an anticipation of what tomorrow might bring, rather than dreading potential negatives.

For myself, I will usually have set days for certain fun routines during the week. Monday will be TV night with a best friend. Tuesday is $5 matinee day at my local theatre. Wednesday, I check out the new books that came out that week at the bookstore, along with my traditional apple tart from the bookstore coffee shop, and so on. Yes, my daughter is grown now, but even if kids are a distraction from such routines, it doesn't change the fact that you will still need to carve out some oases for yourself.

Typically, it's best to have some oases that are in the immediate future and others that are more in the distance. I usually plan at least one big trip a year to somewhere I've never been, and a few smaller weekend trips during the spring and fall.

If you already have positive routines in place, you still need to look at them from time to time, because sometimes they can become *too* routine – losing their effectiveness. It's necessary at times to break up the routines, making life a little more interesting (and maybe a little more meaningful), helping you to connect more with the world around you, and stepping out of your comfort zone.

The biggest benefit of finding and valuing the continuing positives in your life is how it breaks the hold the negative has on you. It makes you more consciously aware of how your brain has gotten into this negative mindset, and how you've continued to create that rut for your thoughts to follow. Time to carve a better path; and all it takes is developing a daily practice of identifying what's still working in your life and what you can do to add more positives to look forward to.

Bullet Points:

- **There are four elements that a personal crisis impacts: body (physical), mind (mental), heart (emotional) and spirit.**

- Maintaining our physical health makes us more resistant to stress and crisis.

- Exercise during crisis is a necessary lifeline.

- Sufficient sleep is crucial.

- Yoga is one of the best forms of exercise for learning how to breathe, how to direct your focus, and how to self-regulate.

- Breathing regulates many of our body's internal systems, moving us towards feeling calm or stressed.

- Mindfulness is being self-aware of our current actions, thoughts, feelings, and our state of tension or relaxation.

- Mindfulness is also being aware and respectful of the thoughts and feelings of others.

- Mindfulness is not being overly mindful of your negative thoughts.

- Thought distortions negatively impact our perspective, biasing how we are seeing our circumstances and relationships.

- To balance the negative, we need to foster an attitude of gratitude, intentionally taking into account the positives that still exist even in the middle of crisis.

- We need to intentionally create positive activities and routines to look forward to; putting revitalizing oases on the horizon that allow us to experience positive expectations of the future.

Discussion Questions:

1. When stress or emotional distress starts to get out of control for you, where does it show itself the most? (Physically, mentally, emotionally, and/or spiritually)

2. How are you doing with maintaining your physical health (diet, exercise and sleep)? What needs improvement and what will that require? If you've been successful with maintaining any of those (diet, exercise, sleep), what's been the key? Would that same key be applicable to the ones that still need improving?

3. Do you use relaxation exercises, breathing techniques and exercise to self-regulate? Do you understand the benefit of yoga? Have you ever tried it? If not, what's kept you from doing it?

4. In terms of the mental, have you ever been accused in any of your relationships (past or present) of distorted thinking? If so, has there been a recurrent theme across relationships (being accused of the same type of distortion by different people)? When approaching crisis, do you recognize any particular distortions that start to occur for you that are hard to let go of? Are there any distortions from the list I gave that you struggle with? If so, what would the undistorted thinking look like? Has there been anyone, or anything, in the past that has helped you correct a distortion of your own? If so, how did they accomplish that?

5. How mindful do you think you are – too little, just right, or too much? If not "just right", what do you need to do different in order to get there? Do you bring mindfulness into your relationships, or is it easy for you to become reactive quickly?

6. Do you practice an attitude of gratitude on a regular basis? Has your focus turned more towards the negative? If so, what do you need to do to start redirecting your thoughts to what's still working in your life, and finding the positives in others?

7. Do you understand the difference between conviction and condemnation? Which do you tend to use more with others? Which do you tend to use most with yourself? If you were globally using just conviction to inspire change, what would you be doing differently?

8. Do you create oases for yourself? Do you see their benefit? Do you have any particular positive routines in the present that you look forward to? Are there any positive routines from your past that you need to bring back to the present?

Chapter 9
When Feelings Dictate

Much of this chapter comes from the solution model I used in my first book on relationship conflict. The basic concept behind the model is that for any personal problem there are potentially three different layers that need attention. That doesn't mean that *every* problem involves all three layers. It just depends on how deep the problem goes.

It's an efficiently structured way to organize an issue and come up with some solution-focused alternatives. It's also a nice way for me to demonstrate how people get things backwards when it comes to dealing with their emotions.

Behavior

The first layer, and usually the easiest to address, is the *behavior* that you engage in that contributes to the problem.

Let's say in this case the identified problem is that a woman in her late 50's has lost her partner to a terminal illness, and a year later she still doesn't seem to be adjusting well. Her identity was all wrapped up in that relationship. Her kids are grown and moved away. She's been isolating herself from friends because she doesn't want to burden them with her sadness, and she doesn't want people to see that she hasn't been taking care of herself – having gained some weight and feeling unattractive. While she's able to live off of the money from her deceased partner's life insurance, it isn't a lot, so she is hesitant to do anything fun that has a price tag attached. She hasn't had a job of her own for several years and feels insecure about starting back. Alone at home, she has started drinking more wine than she normally would and watches whatever's on TV to pass the time, often falling asleep in her living room chair before bedtime. Her normal hobbies (reading, hiking, music) are no longer enjoyable to her because all of those things she connects to doing with her partner present. Getting out of the house by herself only makes her feel more alone.

She is showing many of the symptoms of depression, and failing to see that if she keeps doing what she's doing she's going to reach a personal crisis point, if she's not already there. The initial crisis may have been situational (the death of her partner), but the next crisis will be a self-created one.

Usually, *even if a problem behavior is self-destructive there is still an underlying legitimate need that is fueling it, no matter how ineffectively.* In this case, *none* of her core needs (security, significance and fun) are now being successfully met. Overeating, drinking alcohol (self-medication), and watching too much TV are attempts at need satisfaction, but they are just Band-Aids for her wound. She had become overly dependent on her partner to satisfy her needs, and without someone else in her life to make those things happen for her, she doesn't know what to do. So now she is practicing helplessness. She is displaying an external locus of control, either waiting for something outside of herself to happen and make her life better again, or possibly she has given up hope that her life will ever be good again.

When finding a solution for problematic behavior, we're simply taking the problem behavior and replacing it with a more ideal behavior that more effectively satisfies the underlying need. In this case, most of her initial loss was relational, so restoring her relationships will be one of the most effective places to start. She needs to be calling and visiting her kids more, inviting her friends over, getting out of the house with friends, maybe finding some new friends, and maybe joining a grief support group or local seniors group or social club.

One mistake people make in these situations (that luckily this woman isn't) is that they try to replace one partner with another, jumping too quickly into another romantic relationship rather than learning how to be alone again. She needs to restore a sense of self-confidence and independence as well as re-establishing her own identity separate from someone else. For this woman, it would be very easy for her to latch on to someone else she could be dependent on, but that really wouldn't solve the problem, it would just mask it.

Remembering balanced priorities, she also needs to start taking better care of her health (better diet, less alcohol, more exercise), possibly finding at least a part-time job, reattempting her hobbies (or finding some new ones), and braving getting out of the house and doing some things on her own.

A job would have several benefits. It would help her self-worth that she was visibly accomplishing something and able to feel productive (significance), and it would also address her need for greater security, being able to afford to do the things she wanted to without fear of overspending.

As far as reclaiming her hobbies, while some people will duplicate the routines of a past relationship as a way to memorialize it, others will go the opposite direction and give up all of the routines that were connected to the other person. The problem with this (giving everything up) is that it's allowing that past relationship to dictate what stays and goes in your life, giving it too much control in the present. If you are reinventing yourself that doesn't mean you're doing it from scratch. You are first trying to think through what you already know you like (what is an authentic fit for you), and deciding to keep it, regardless of who it might have been connected to. In doing so, you are reclaiming a positive part of you that doesn't need to be sacrificed. By this woman giving up so many of her personal interests, she was losing even more of herself in the process.

The twin mentality is a reflection of this, where one sibling gives up an interest, or a hairstyle, or a relationship, just because their counterpart likes the same thing. They think they are creating their own uniqueness by doing this, but they are still allowing the other to dictate their choices based on what has already been picked.

No doubt, if this woman looked at those new options all at once, she would feel overwhelmed. But she doesn't have to attempt everything all at once. She would just start with a few at a time, breaking them down into the first doable steps for the upcoming week, and build on them from there.

On the simplest level, replacing a negative behavior with a positive one that better satisfies the underlying need can be all the solution one needs. But, many times, the problem goes deeper than just the behavior, in which case we need to look at the next layer as well.

Thinking

The second layer to the solution model is our *thinking*.

It is the thoughts that we tell ourselves (our self-talk) that creates, nurtures or maintains the problem. Whether it's denial that we've got a problem, minimizing the problem, or how we rationalize continuing to engage in the problem, our problematic way of thinking can allow the problem to persist.

We often feel things because of what we intentionally or unintentionally choose to tell ourselves. It makes perfect sense that if I tell myself an anxious thought, I am going to have an anxious reaction. But, for many, they aren't aware of their self-talk, they just know how they felt as a result of it. Once they can start to recognize all of the negative things that they tell themselves that shape their emotions, and start to realize that they are just as capable of telling themselves something positive (that there's a choice), they start taking back control.

I like to use the example of two people on a rollercoaster ride. One freaks out when they get to the top of the biggest drop and start to go down, feeling terrified. The person sitting beside them, sharing the very same experience, has a completely different interpretation, finding the experience thrilling. They both have the same internal excited body response (heart rate increase, breathing changes, physical tension), but each tells themselves two different things about what they were experiencing. One interprets it as, "I'm afraid". The other interprets it as, "I'm excited." They each made an unconscious choice which determined whether or not they'd get back on a rollercoaster again.

Along these lines, narrative therapy is a form of counseling that looks at the stories that make up our lives, and the meaning we've attached to those stories. Sometimes the problem isn't what happened to us, but our interpretation of what happened. When we can reframe the experience (Chapter 5), allowing for other meanings or interpretations, rather than only the one that's been holding us back for so long, we sometimes find new freedom.

◆　◆　◆

Problematic thinking usually starts with just a truthful observation, neither good nor bad, which progressively deteriorates into a distortion, emotional logic, or a conspiracy theory.

For this woman, it may just start with the awareness of, "I'm alone now." Which is true, she is. From there, if her thinking is problematic, it will deteriorate into more painful thoughts and assumptions. "I've never been alone before." "I don't know if I can do this on my own." "I don't know what to do." "I don't have any energy." "This feels overwhelming."

There's often a progression from considering the possibility of what *might* happen that now becomes a conclusion of what *will* happen – so now it's a negative *belief*. "I don't know if I can do this on my own," becomes, "I can't do this on my own."

The initial step with thinking is just tracking the different problematic thought trails we engage in that justify our continued problematic behavior. Past that point, we then need to come up with positive counters, or redirects, to those thoughts that will help empower us to follow through on the ideal behaviors we've already identified.

We don't want to create redirects that are too idealistic or unrealistic, just positive counters that restore hope and direction. "One step at a time; I can do this." "I need to reach out to my friends; that's what they're there for. I don't have to be completely alone." "It may feel overwhelming, but I don't have to do everything at once." "I'm not going to get more energy by sitting around." "I need to start bringing some positives back into my life." "I can't let my feelings dictate what I do."

This is also where identifying and using our personal mantras comes into play, using those phrases that symbolize a greater positive concept or meaning, helping us to stay focused. "Baby steps." "One day at a time." "Keep it simple."

Many times, we will depend on our friends to help talk us through things, which is fine so long as we don't become dependent on them for this. By relying solely on other people to move us through discomfort or distress, we are unintentionally confirming that we can't do it for ourselves.

By being able to identify the most powerful redirects, the ones that work the best for us, we are collecting tools for our own toolbox that don't depend on others being present to help us refocus.

If the problem doesn't go any deeper, and both unhealthy thoughts and behaviors are consistently managed and positively redirected, the situation usually starts to self-correct.

If a problem *still* persists, despite sound behavioral and cognitive interventions, it's probably because it goes to the third layer. The third aspect to the solution model is the feelings themselves.

Feelings (the Fire Element)

Last chapter I started to talk about the four elements/aspects of overall health (body, mind, heart and spirit). Heart, the third aspect, is the realm of our *emotions*. Its corresponding element is fire. Similar to fire, our feelings can be in a constant state of flux and become quite destructive if left unchecked. However, just as a well-tended fire on a cold winter night can be both lifesaving and soothing, feelings (when both nurtured and guided) can positively enhance every aspect of our lives. While feelings can add to (or create) a crisis, they can also help pull us out of one.

When attempting to intellectually self-soothe in the midst of emotional distress, our feelings get in the way because, by their nature, they are not rooted in reason, and, when escalated, can be beyond reason.

When we say that we feel conflicted, typically the conflict is between what we think versus what we feel (two different parts of the brain). We may know that what we feel is unreasonable, yet still be unable to give up feeling it. We may logically know that our behavior is irrational, yet still have difficulty doing something different.

Returning to the current example of the lonely widow, her primary feelings at this point would most likely be a mix of sadness, loneliness, despair, fear, dread, and insecurity – lost.

When feelings are a big part of the problem there is often a circular dynamic that occurs between what we feel and what we do, and thinking starts to take a backseat. It's not that we stop thinking completely, but our focus is more on the emotions than the thoughts that affect them. She feels depressed and without energy, so she does nothing. She feels anxious about starting a new job, so she doesn't look for one. What thinking is still conscious is now mostly short-term thinking, either rehashing how bad she feels or what she needs to do to get immediate relief from what she's feeling – get a glass of wine, eat something, turn on the TV. So the feelings are now dictating her choices.

To become more solution-focused, she needs to start thinking long-term again. "If I do this (drink, eat, watch TV), how is that getting me any closer to feeling alive again?" "Is what I'm doing actually making things any better?" "What do I need to do to start getting past this?"

The difficulty with the feeling aspect, moreso than the other two layers, is that *you can't just replace a negative feeling with a better one.* I can replace a negative behavior with a positive one, or an unhealthy thought with a healthier one, but I can't just get up in the morning feeling lousy and tell myself to be happy. I'm going to have to *do* something, or start *thinking* about something, that allows my emotions to shift. *With emotional discipline, we guide our feelings to where we want them to be through positive action and thought, rather than the other way around.*

When it comes to weakening unhealthy, negative emotions and irrational beliefs, *you have to be willing to live in a way that challenges their truth.*

For this woman, despite her job anxiety, she needs to start getting information about what jobs are available and start applying, just to see what bites she gets. Just by taking small steps towards getting a job, she is weakening the hold anxiety has on her that says, "I can't do it". If she's afraid of failing, she needs to prove to herself that she can succeed. By not trying, she is already failing, undermining whatever self-confidence she has left.

For the depressed individual, they have to start doing the things they would normally be doing if they weren't depressed. The more they cater to the depression, the more depressed they will feel.

So the ideal positive feelings that this woman is trying to create for herself would be re-experiencing joy, companionship, hope, security, and newfound direction. But the only way she's going to get there is through changing her actions and thoughts.

◆　◆　◆

For many, when you first start to implement a plan for change, if the emotions are holding you back, you have to approach it in terms of "fake it to make it", because the negative feelings will still be in the way, sabotaging your efforts. "Fake it to make it" (a 12-step program slogan) doesn't mean to lie to yourself or others. It means that, at the start, while you're trying to make those initial efforts to create a new identity, or restore an old one, *you have to step into the shoes of that successful identity before you're actually feeling it.* The desired feelings don't come first, they come *after.*

For the feelings-based person, that's a difficult concept. It feels more honest to just feel what they feel. But *while feelings can sometimes be useful guides, they are often poor decision-makers*. Our romanticized culture focuses on "go with your heart", which can be a good lead when it comes to choosing a career, but doesn't work well in most other situations since the stronger the emotion the more likely it is that our perception becomes distorted.

◆ ◆ ◆

In guiding your feelings, I'm not suggesting that you try to force an emotion, since this can sabotage the natural workings of your brain. The feelings should be allowed to occur naturally in response to our actions and thoughts. If we are overanalyzing ourselves for their presence or absence, we can be interrupting that natural flow. Our focus needs to be on the doing and the thinking, trusting that the feelings will follow in time.

If you accomplish a goal, the feelings of accomplishment come after, not before. Yes, we will likely get some degree of satisfaction just working towards that goal, but the sense of completion only occurs when it's done.

Forcing feelings is similar to how some forms of insomnia develop. Our body already knows how to fall asleep, if we just let it. But the more it becomes an intentional process, trying to force sleep to occur, the more we're getting in the way of it actually happening. We are trying to overly control a natural process, so now it's no longer natural.

◆ ◆ ◆

One of the strategies used with communication is the tool of learning how to ask good *questions*. Most couples who have unhealthy patterns of arguing no longer take the time to ask questions. They are focused mostly on making *statements* about 1) how they feel or think, or 2) what kind of a person they feel or think their partner is, or 3) what they think their partner feels or thinks, or 4) what they think their partner should do differently.

Useful questions actually help de-escalate extreme emotions because, if the partner is to engage the question, actually think it through, then they have to let go of some of their agitation. (Remember, we can't fully feel and think at the same time – one is going to dominate.) The more I move my partner into thinking things through by asking sincere, probing questions, the more their emotion now falls into the background, increasing the odds of being able to have a more reasonable, adult conversation.

My point here is that the same thing works when we ask ourselves healthy questions. The more we fully engage the question, the more problematic emotion recedes. "Which of my tools would be most effective in this moment?" "Rather than being problem-obsessed, what would be a good solution for resolving how I'm feeling?" "Rather than just continuing to do what I've proven already doesn't work, what might be a better choice?"

◆ ◆ ◆

So, while this is a 3-part solution model, there are really only two interventions: behavior and thinking. Is one more effective than the other? Both have their place, but it usually depends on the particular person and the situation.

Because strong emotions and irrational beliefs are, by definition, *beyond* reason, trying to reason with them in the heat of the moment sometimes isn't as effective as simply doing something positive that breaks us out of their control.

Many times people will *overthink* a situation and talk themselves out of doing something healthy. So they may need to adopt the Nike slogan of "Just do it" (another possible mantra) and not give themselves any more time to think, since "thinking" for them just means becoming emotionally overwhelmed. Their strategy of choice for those times would be *behavioral*.

On the other hand, for those caught in the spiral of the feelings dictating the choices, because often there is an absence of rational thought going on, their focus should be on learning better *thinking* strategies that restore a big-picture perspective to their situation and a heightened awareness of the consequences of their immediate choices.

Embracing the Feeling

Stepping back from the solution model I just went through, there is an initial path to consider in dealing with feelings, *before* it becomes necessary to guide them through action and thought. That first step is to allow ourselves to actually embrace the uncomfortable emotion. While that may sound masochistic, it's more about learning to not fear what we label as negative emotions. Part of being human is just being able to feel what we feel. If we have this whole range of negative emotions (anxiety, guilt, shame, sadness, etc.) that we actively avoid or repress, then we are also suppressing part of being human, and we don't learn how to get more comfortable with having discomfort.

For people who are more feelings-based, feelings come and go. The emotions that they experience, comfortable or uncomfortable, are familiar and more easily accepted as just what they are feeling in that moment. While many feelings-based people still need to learn emotional regulation (so that the feelings don't dictate everything that they do), they usually don't fear uncomfortable emotions as much as thinking-based individuals do.

For thinking-based people, uncomfortable emotions threaten their internal control. Because they are not usually ruled by their emotions, when the emotions start to misbehave, they are less likely to know how to handle them, other than to redouble their efforts to put the emotions back in their place. When they enter crisis (the emotions now out of control), the crisis is magnified because of their lack of experience with knowing how to handle being emotionally flooded.

Feelings are just feelings. Their power is only what we give to them. If I'm in crisis, I can be sitting in my living room thinking how unbearable it is to be in my house by myself. I may feel compelled to seek out others to be around so that I don't feel so isolated. My home becomes representative of being alone, so I no longer look forward to going home. But the reality, beyond the feelings, is that the living room is neither good nor bad, it's just a room. My sitting there is neither good nor bad, it's just me sitting.

If I'm able to move past the feelings, my situation becomes normalized again – just me sitting at home in my living room, nothing unbearable about it. Everything that made that experience unbearable for me was all in my head.

The approach of embracing your feelings instead of just managing them is partly to restore an acceptance of all the aspects of being human, not just the parts you're most comfortable with; it's a movement towards wholeness. But it's also understanding that part of moving past uncomfortable emotions isn't to keep them at a distance, where they still exist, waiting on the outskirts, but to allow them in – to be acknowledged and experienced, explored and accepted as part of who you are.

It's the exploration and acceptance pieces that are the most important. Exploring your emotions helps you better understand yourself and why you feel the way you feel. Exploration can lead to identifying solutions that will resolve the reason for the uncomfortable feeling's existence in the first place.

Acceptance often moves us closer to "it is what it is". When we've experienced a significant loss, acceptance is the light at the end of the tunnel – us moving forward once again.

When we get to the point where we allow ourselves to feel what we feel, without dreading or repressing it, the feeling is likely to move on more quickly than take up residence, because it's finally been acknowledged and accepted.

"This is a depressing situation. It makes perfect sense that I'd feel depressed right now."

"That relationship really meant a lot to me. If I didn't care about them, it wouldn't hurt as much as it does. I can at least feel good that I really did care."

"That really did feel like a loss. I don't have to act like it didn't. And it's okay to allow myself to feel it, rather than just rush through it or push it away."

Paradoxical Intent

There is also a therapy technique sometimes used called *paradoxical intent*, which uses a similar approach but for a different reason. Here again, the uncomfortable emotion becomes the prescription. In other words, "I want you to set aside fifteen minutes tonight to be anxious" (or depressed, or whatever the uncomfortable emotion is). And, again, that probably sounds masochistic.

In this instance, though, it's not about embracing how you feel, it's about forcing the feeling. Remember what I said about forcing emotions? The more you try to force them, the more you interrupt the natural process of experiencing them on an emotional level. So the more you try to intellectually make it happen, you weaken the emotional experience and the hold that is has on you. Because you are now choosing it, rather than fearing when it's going to show up next, it can change the emotional dynamic.

You probably wouldn't want to attempt this if you hadn't already explored and worked through some of the emotions, because then this could just be another form of emotional suppression. However, if you've already done the emotional work, then it can be a simple tool for shortcircuiting the feelings when they present themselves at inopportune times.

◆　◆　◆

Much of successful counseling simply has to do with helping a client become more conscious of what they do, why they do it, and finding better alternatives for them that actually work. The more self-aware they are, the better they can make intentional choices with both their actions and their thoughts; learning to both embrace and guide their feelings along better paths.

Bullet Points:

- **There are potentially three aspects to every personal issue: the behavior, the thinking, and the feeling.**

- Often there is an underlying need we are trying to meet with the things that we do, we just may be going about it in an unhealthy way. We are always trying to say, "Yes" to the underlying need – just finding better, balanced, non-destructive ways to do so.

- With behavior, we are trying to replace the problem behaviors with more ideal behaviors that better satisfy the underlying need.

- With thinking, we are trying to replace the problem thinking with more positive redirects that support the desired behavior.

- With feeling, we can't change how we feel by willing it. We have to do something positive or think something positive (or both) in order for our feelings to shift.

- Emotions can be the most complicated to deal with because, when extreme, they are beyond reason.

- Chronic negative feelings and irrational beliefs, even with behavioral and cognitive change, are not likely to go away overnight. But every time we are successful in redirecting them, not catering to them, we weaken them rather than feed them.

- For someone struggling with lack of emotional discipline, the feelings dictate the choices. Someone who is emotionally disciplined, guides their feelings through their actions and thought.

- "Fake it to make it" applies when we are trying to make better choices even though our emotions aren't supporting our efforts.

- Sometimes letting ourselves feel what we feel, even if it's negative, allows the feelings to move on rather than take up residence.

• **Paradoxical intent is where we intentionally choose to engage more in the problematic emotion, paradoxically taking away its power because we're *choosing* to do it rather than feeling helpless that we can't stop doing it.**

3-Part Solution Exercise:

1) Take two separate pieces of paper. Divide each sheet into three sections: behavior, thinking and feeling. Identify a specific problem that you're struggling with. The first sheet represents you in the present. The second sheet represents the ideal, what you're working towards.

2) What are the *behaviors* that occur that either are part of the problem or resulting from the problem? For example, if the identified problem is getting angry, the behaviors that go along with that might be "I say cruel things", "I lecture", or "I'll be mean to the kids" or "I withdraw". List them on the first sheet under the behavior section. Try to be as specific as possible.

3) What are the specific *thoughts* you have that are either creating the issue or contributing to the issue? Usually, the first thought in the chain is just an *observation* (without interpretation, assumption or judgment). For instance, "He didn't take out the garbage again" is just an observation. But it may then lead to, "Once again he didn't do what he said that he would do", which might lead to, "It really bothers me that I can't count on him", which might lead to "If he cared about me, he wouldn't be doing this." Write the whole train of thought that goes along with the problem on the first page under the thinking section. Feel free to track as many "trains" as are connected to the particular problem.

(You may need to track the thought process backwards, starting at the most conscious problem thought and then tracking it back to the initial neutral observation.)

4) What *feelings* continue to occur that are complicating things? Continuing with the example just given, the feelings might be: anxious, depressed, sad, lonely, unloved, disrespected, betrayed, angry, disappointed, neglected, etc. Write down whatever your feelings are that are related to, or driving, the problem.

5) See if you can identify the need or needs that you've been trying to meet for yourself by doing what you've been doing – even if it hasn't worked. Remember that our core needs are all the same: security, significance and fun.

6) The second page represents the ideal. It's what you're aiming towards; what the desired situation would be.

   Starting with the behavior category, write down the positive *behaviors* that you need to be doing to replace the current negative ones you've already listed. In this instance, it might be, "Try to educate him in a non-lecture way that this isn't about the trash; it's about him keeping his word.", "Letting him know I feel like I'm unimportant to him, rather than attacking him (talking from the hurt and not the anger)", "Let the minor things go", "Controlling my temper". Try to think of as many positive alternative behaviors as you can. The more options you have the better. Once you're done, look at whether these behaviors would successfully satisfy the need you've identified, even if just in part. If they're still not satisfying the need, see if you can come up with better behavioral options that would.

7) Go to the ideal thought section (second page). What *thoughts* would effectively counter the problem thinking? For instance, "The garbage being taken out when I want it to is my preference, not a need – not worth getting that upset about," "He does show me in other ways that he cares". The ideal positive thoughts you're coming up with need to be thoughts you can embrace because they are credible for you and have weight. Don't list thoughts that you really can't buy into. They need to be ideas that, when you

consider them, effectively de-escalate where your feelings would take you.

8) Lastly, list the feelings that would be desired. In this instance, the feelings might be, "I want to feel valued", "I want to feel like I have some control over what gets done", "I want to feel like everything doesn't depend on me".

9) Having completed the pages, I sometimes suggest getting rid of the first one. It served as the template for establishing what you're working towards, but your focus now needs to be on the ideal you're trying to create. The second chart becomes your gauge at the end of each day as to how well you've progressed towards making that picture a reality. And it serves as a reminder of the things you can do and think about when you're being tempted to backslide or are feeling distant from remembering your alternatives.

The model can be used with individual problems or relational problems. If you do the exercise as a couple, you'd need a set for each person's part of the problem.

Often, the easiest sections to fill out are the ones which that person is the most "in touch" with about themselves (actions, thoughts, feelings). The parts that are hardest to fill in are usually that person's particular blind spot.

Chapter 10
Spirituality

The fourth, and final, aspect/element of overall health is *spirit*. Similar to air, we can't see it, but we can see evidence of its existence (as with the movement of the wind) whenever we encounter the miraculous in life, or when events go beyond any explainable coincidence.

While spirituality doesn't have to be wrapped up in a particular faith, it can enhance whatever faith you already practice (if you have one). In part, it is a reflection of the *depth* of your faith, and, if active, would be reflected in your actual lifestyle. It's not religiosity, which is simply measured by how much you practice the rituals of a particular religion, with no assurance of any depth or it actually being applied to the external world.

Spirituality is one primary aspect of how we find meaning and purpose in life, and how we try to answer the existential questions of "Why am I here?", "What should I be doing with my life?", "What actually matters?", and "What's the point of living?". It's how we go about taking into consideration life beyond ourselves, life beyond the limits of the end of our own life, and life beyond the physical world.

When we don't have good enough answers to some of those questions, we will typically experience *existential anxiety* because, being human and self-aware, we have an inborn need for meaning and purpose – some direction for our lives. When we look at midlife crises, or a major loss such as the death of a loved one, or some of the major transitions in life (such as entering old age), an existential crisis is predictable. Those forced shifts make us reassess how we've been choosing to live our lives, and how much of what we've done (or are doing) actually matters.

Ideally, a healthy belief system provides some additional tools to move through a personal crisis. Yet, it's surprising how often those in personal crisis, even though they have a personal belief system, will still fail to think of using the tools that their specific faith provides.

When we look at the mind-boggling intricacies of the natural world and the universe, even the personal experiences we may have had in our own lives that go beyond coincidence; it becomes very difficult to attribute it all to random chance. There is a natural order to things that supports the concept of a greater design to existence.

For many, life consists of going through stepping-stone experiences that, looking back on it, helped prepare them for the tests and struggles that occurred later in life. It's as if there was a greater wisdom at work, moving them along, helping them in their development.

The reality is that we will never know the answers to all of life's questions in this lifetime, so, to some degree, we each have to also learn to embrace mystery for the things we can only guess at, and be tolerant of how others try to come up with answers for those mysteries. But some of those mysteries, if we're paying attention, may actually get answered as we go on with our lives, to the degree that we can start to practice the principles that we learn that come out of those experiences.

For example, if we start to practice living by faith (sometimes defined as "confidence in what we hope for and assurance about what we do not see") then we are consciously projecting a positive future outcome. By walking in that faith, we are more likely to see the positives that exist as we go forward and even create more positives, because that is how we are now choosing to live.

Faith and action go hand in hand. If there are no steps taken to live out our faith, then we're just engaged in positive thinking. While positive thinking can grant us temporary mental and emotional relief, ultimately, it is our actions that make more of a visible difference in the world around us. I can believe in a better world, but if I'm not taking steps to make that happen, then I'm practicing an empty faith through wishful thinking.

♦ ♦ ♦

"What should I be doing with my life?" is the typical question we ask ourselves when first trying to figure out how we're going to make enough money to live on our own. At that early point in our life when we're just seeking our own independence, the question is only looking at the physical world, not the spiritual.

Some people are lucky enough to find a job that they are passionate about. Others are lucky enough to find a job that they're good at. Most have to initially be okay with just making a paycheck.

As we get older, however, that same question ("What should I be doing with my life?") is no longer about income, it becomes about meaning and purpose. For those whose jobs don't also fulfill their need for meaning and purpose, they will have to either consider finding a different line of work, or find meaning and purpose outside of their work if they want to experience contentment.

Even those who have need-fulfilling jobs, at different points in time should probably question if the need-fulfillment is authentic or artificial. We can feel both secure and significant with the work that we do even when what we are doing doesn't actually make a positive difference or serve any meaningful purpose for anyone other than ourselves and our employers. But thinking only of ourselves, and our family, can start feeling somewhat limited and shortsighted the more we age. As a result, many will become more involved in their community, their faith, politics, charities and volunteer activities as they mature. Giving back and making a lasting difference becomes more of an intentional focus.

Those who experience a midlife crisis are typically struggling with these questions. They may have been living a life that was laid out for them by what others told them they should do, or based on what they were good at, but now that they have had more time to learn who they really are, they may realize that what they've been doing doesn't actually fit with who they've become or what they believe. If they don't have the freedom at that point to make the necessary changes for a better fit, then it presents a dilemma.

While age and maturity will move us to wrestle with these questions (and hopefully find authentic solutions), ideally we don't wait until most of our life has already passed to figure these things out, or we will also be struggling with regret. The younger we are when we take these things into account, the better we'll feel about the life that we've lived.

Mature versus Rigid Belief Systems

For the person whose life is in crisis, religion can provide a meaningful path to experiencing relief. However, there is the concern in these situations that, if their need is too great or they don't have enough of a developed sense of self, they run the risk that they will develop an overly rigid belief system.

If it's a rigid faith, there is often the outward appearance of being overly certain about what they now say that they believe, but it can actually be a very fragile faith because, inwardly, they are easily threatened by the questions of others. Such people, afraid of losing their internal security, remain closed to new information. As a result, there may be little room for actual growth.

The same can be said for the atheist whose security comes from the rigidity with which they hang on to their disbelief. The thought of an afterlife, with an actual God or gods, can sometimes be scarier than a universe without. At times, their rigidity comes from having been disappointed or scarred by past experiences with religion (or religious persons). That's unfortunate, because it means their rejection of a personal faith was a reactive one, not a researched one.

With mature spirituality, there is a questing aspect to how we are looking to learn from life and interact with life around us in meaningful ways. As we form our theories about meaning and purpose in life, and have some of the blanks filled in as we gain knowledge and experience, we will also have times when we need to take a step back and change some of the ways we do or think about things when we find that some of our conclusions were incorrect. This practice of flexibility, learning and correcting, shapes us to be more open to necessary change and, as a result, better prepared to deal with the changes that crises sometimes require.

◆　◆　◆

What you *believe* is at the core of who you are, and is very resistant to change. It is different from what you *think*, which is more about facts, information and opinions. You can change a person's *opinion* with new information. A belief system, even with new information, is more resistant because it's so deeply imbedded in how that person views the world. If someone changes his religion, or is able to compromise his "beliefs" with little effort, it's typically because he hadn't truly internalized them to start with.

Scott Peck ("The Road Less Traveled") believed that there are 4 stages to spiritual growth.

Stage 1 is essentially pre-faith. The individual has committed to no spiritual beliefs and is pretty much self-centered. Life is limited to what's in front of the eyes.

Stage 2 is engaging in an organized religion, where the personal understanding is relatively simplified, such as between good and evil, with an attitude of blind compliance to whatever the rituals and teachings may be. (Peck thought that the majority of the world's population stays in Stage 2.)

Stage 3 is where the individual experiences a crisis of faith. They start to step away from the conventional thinking and begin asking questions, challenging what they thought they knew and what they've been taught. Peck didn't see this as a step backward, but a step forward. It wasn't retreating into narcissism and chaos; it was challenging pre-conceived ideas which, ideally, if pursued and allowed to progress, would go deeper to finding one's own true identity and faith.

Stage 4 is where the individual arrives at a mature faith, because it's no longer a borrowed, institutionalized or unexamined one. There is still room for the unknown, and a willingness to embrace mystery. Teaching isn't embraced blindly, nor is there compliance out of fear of judgment or rejection. It involves coming to a deeper, healthy love for others, and a better application of spiritual concepts such as faith, forgiveness, repentance and grace.

◆ ◆ ◆

In Chapter 6, I mentioned that I was raised in a family that went to a Presbyterian church. So I was raised Christian. In my teens, my parents left the Presbyterian church and went non-denominational, meaning that they didn't believe that any one denomination had it perfectly right.

One of the best lessons I learned from them came from when I would sit in the back seat of the car after church, headed somewhere for lunch, listening to them debate whatever the message had been. My parents weren't respecters of titles or degrees; they were respecters of knowledge and competence. Through their conversations, they taught me critical thinking – how to think for myself. They essentially gave me permission to ask questions rather than accept what I was told just because somebody or something claimed it was true. In a world where the majority look to be led rather than to lead, and where so many are overly dependent on information that comes from social media, critical thinking is crucial.

This played out later in my life when, as a young adult just starting grad school, I decided that I needed to think through what I had been raised to believe and make sure that it was an authentic fit for myself. As much as possible, I wanted to start from scratch, in order for it to be an unbiased process. So I started going to the library and reading through the different world religions. In part, I also wanted to do this so I could come from a position of knowledge in talking to people of differing faiths, having done the work of coming to know and understand their perspective.

It took about a year, but I finally decided to return to Christianity as my own choice, not because it was how I was raised or what was most familiar, but because it resonated the most with my own life experience up to that point. Moving forward, it was easier for me to explore Christianity because it was now my conscious choice, not something I had just adopted or what my parents wanted me to do.

Similar to going through a midlife crisis, it's important for everyone at different points in their life to take the time to go deeper with why they believe what they believe, why they do what they do, and ask themselves if it's still a good fit. Does it actually work in practice? Also, is how they live their life actually consistent with what they say they believe, and, if not, what's going to change – the lifestyle or the belief? Is their faith a comfort but ultimately stagnant because there's no further exploration or continued growth to it? What would developing it further look like?

It's choosing to live a very conscious life, rather than just getting through the day letting life (and others) make the decisions for you (which it will, if you let it). The more authentic the fit between you and the life that you choose, and the more consistent the practice between what you do and what you believe, the more centered and at peace you will feel.

Specific faiths

Most faiths are made up of 1) a core doctrine (wisdom, moral teaching, and lifestyle instruction), 2) some aspect of prayer or meditation, and 3) the support that comes from being part of a community of fellow believers. Yes, that can also be true for a cult, but cults are more easily recognized by how they attempt to overly control the information their followers have access to, and controlling the followers themselves.

For those faiths that promote the existence of a positive afterlife, there is predictable relief for those overly concerned about death as a worst-case scenario. But, hopefully, we're not choosing a faith based just on the convenience of its teachings, rather the evidence of its truths.

Core doctrine usually provides instruction for how to deal with life's stressors. If it's a healthy faith, taught in an effective way, the quality of one's personal life, and one's ability to cope with life, should improve. The teachings that come out of the core doctrine are usually filled with wise sayings that, if actually taken and applied to one's life, can restore or add to one's moral compass, and also provide more gems to add to one's personal list of meaningful mantras.

Here's a few that come to mind from mine, regarding crisis:

"Who of you by worrying can add a single hour to his life? ... Therefore do not worry about tomorrow, for tomorrow will worry about itself. Each day has enough trouble of its own." – Matthew 6:27, 34 (NIV)

"Consider it pure joy, my brothers and sisters, whenever you face trials of many kinds, because you know that the testing of your faith produces perseverance. Let perseverance finish its work so that you may be mature and complete, not lacking anything." – James 1: 2-4 (NIV)

"...whatever is true, whatever is noble, whatever is right, whatever is pure, whatever is lovely, whatever is admirable – if anything is excellent or praiseworthy – think about such things." – Philippians 4:8 (NIV)

"Do not be anxious about anything, but in every situation, by prayer and petition, with thanksgiving, present your requests to God." – Philippians 4:6 (NIV)

"Cast all your anxiety on Him because He cares for you." – I Peter 5:7 (NIV)

"Come to me, all you who are weary and burdened, and I will give you rest. Take my yoke upon you and learn from me, for I am gentle and humble in heart, and you will find rest for your souls. For my yoke is easy and my burden is light." – Matthew 11:28-30 (NIV)

"If you're not dead, God's not done with you." – various

"If God is your source, what do you have to worry about?" – my Dad

◆　◆　◆

Prayer or meditation provide for time to self-reflect, to practice gratitude, to consider what errors you may have made for which you need to take responsibility, to identify personal needs, to consider the needs of others, and to let go of those things beyond your control – turning them over to whoever your Higher Power is perceived to be. (Even for someone with no personal belief system, knowing how to let go of what's not in your control is critical.)

One of the most well-known prayers that is applicable to personal crises is Reinhold Niebuhr's "Serenity Prayer", used commonly in 12-step groups. The reason it's called the Serenity Prayer is because, if we effectively practice what it teaches, we are much more likely to experience inner peace.

Here is a shortened version:

"God grant me the serenity to accept the things I cannot change; courage to change the things I can; and wisdom to know the difference. Living one day at a time; enjoying one moment at a time; accepting hardships as the pathway to peace."

◆　◆　◆

The presence or absence of *community* can have a large impact on the degree to which we experience crisis. When I went through my divorce many years ago, it was my support group of friends who had gone through similar experiences that served as one of my most important lifelines. That sense of belonging, that "I am not alone", can be a major aid to moving past crisis, combating a sense of isolation.

Just because you are part of a community, though, doesn't guarantee any depth or substance to it. If you can't be real with those people, can't be honest with them and show your true self, then it's not going to be as meaningful.

Choosing a community can have as broad a focus as finding others that value and respect each other's spiritual walk, or it can be as specific as finding just those that share your particular faith. But you probably wouldn't want to be so restrictive that you only chose people who mirrored your own thinking, since there would be nothing to balance or challenge you with those relationships.

Even then, remember that there are safe and unsafe people. Safe people bring a healthy mindset to your relationship with them – they inspire, support and uplift. Unsafe people tend to use other people for their own ends, can be self-absorbed, take more than they give, may be lost in negativity, and hold you back rather than guide you forward. So you have to be selective in both the communities you become a part of, as well as whom you choose to befriend within those communities.

True community is experienced when you have interlaced relationships, where you know they've got your back and you've got theirs. It's knowing that you've got support in both bad times as well as good. If those are healthy relationships, usually there is a sense of both connectedness and progression – that their presence in your life inspires and challenges you to be a better person, and vice versa.

Bullet Points:

- **An active spiritual life, while not having to be attached to a particular religion, adds an extra dimension to our existence, especially in terms of overall meaning and purpose. It also provides additional tools for dealing with personal crises.**

- **Spirituality considers the meaningfulness of the life we're currently living, life beyond ourselves, life beyond the physical, what we leave behind after we pass, and whether or not there is an afterlife. It is measured by the depth of our beliefs and, if active, is reflected in our lifestyle.**

- **Religiosity is measured by the number and frequency of rituals you engage in specific to your faith. Practicing the rituals of a religion does not predict spirituality or depth of faith.**

- A mature belief system remains open to new information.

- A rigid or immature belief system is closed to new information.

- A positive spiritual faith typically consists of: 1) useful wisdom for healthy living and moral guidelines, 2) prayer and/or meditation, and 3) a supportive community that shares a similar belief system and promotes personal growth.

- At some point in life, if we are to live an authentic one, we must review the things we have been taught or adopted, and decide what of that is worth keeping (because it works and is useful), and what we need to leave behind.

Discussion Questions:

1. What is the difference between spirituality and religiosity? Do you consider yourself more spiritual, more religious, or neither? What are the pros and cons of that?

2. If at all spiritual, how is it reflected in your lifestyle and relationships? How does your spirituality help you through, or prevent, crises? Do you remember to apply your spiritual beliefs when you experience emotional distress?

3. What is the difference between a mature versus a rigid belief system? Do you fall into either category? When you think of your friends, do any of them fall into those categories?

4. Does anything prevent you from developing a personal belief system further? If you were to pursue growing or learning more in that way, what would that look like?

5. If you practice a personal faith, does it have a particular doctrine regarding avoiding, preventing or getting through crisis? If so, what does that doctrine teach? Do you apply it?

6. Does your faith involve a form of prayer or meditation? Do you practice it?

7. Are you connected to a group of fellow believers? Do you experience meaningful community with that group? If not, what could you do to create a better sense of community for yourself?

Afterword

When people talk about personal crises, there are three phrases that automatically come to my mind.

1. Crisis often forces necessary change.

I talked about this at the beginning of the book. Sometimes crises occur either because things weren't working the way we were going about it, or a situational crisis is challenging us in a way that we weren't prepared for. During such times, change becomes necessary if we are to start moving out of the crisis, or do a better job of persevering through the crisis. *And often that change needed to happen even if the crisis never did.*

While we don't like emotional discomfort, sometimes significant discomfort is what finally motivates us to do the work of setting things right – making a necessary self-improvement, or getting to a better place with our lives.

2. Crisis can reveal the presence of, or a lack of, character.

In Chapter 7, I talked about how a crisis tends to pull back the layers, revealing our underlying issues.

"Crisis reveals character" is an important thing to remember when we are choosing potential partners or friends since anybody can be nice in good times. So long as no one's rocking the boat, there is the potential illusion that everyone in that boat is a safe person to have on board. But in choosing the people we have in our lives, the people we hope will be there for us when we need them, it's important to be able to see who they are when things aren't going their way. Are they still able to be fair, care about others, be respectful, work towards compromise, take ownership, or does everything quickly become all about them and their pain?

Hopefully, our judgment is balanced in that, while we do make note of what particular negatives surface, we are still able to recognize that what we are seeing is a person in crisis, and not necessarily the sum of who they are.

So, too, it may not be until a crisis occurs that we can clearly see our own baggage and weak spots. In that respect, crises can be both humbling and enlightening.

3. Crisis can create character.

While it's true that people who have gone through a lot can become hardened in a not-so-good way, it's also true that sometimes the people who have gone through the most have the most developed character. They allowed those hardships to refine them, learned from them, grew from them, rather than becoming bitter and closed off. In those instances, a crisis can be positively transformative.

Rather than fearing all of the possible things that may go wrong in life, we can reframe the experience by accepting that part of living involves predictable struggles. But those struggles are opportunities for us to grow, challenging us to adapt. They are only wasted experiences if we fail to learn from them.

You may doubt your ability to handle painful situations, but, just like a good physical trainer will prove to you, *you're stronger than you think.*

Potential crises are then no longer about fear of drowning, tossed about by our own emotional waves, but focusing on learning how to swim, teaching ourselves how to ride the waves back to calmer waters.

It's remembering, too, that there are a lot of other people with us in this ocean that are also learning, or have already learned, the same skills. So, *you're not alone*, but sometimes you have to look around for an assist, and sometimes you need to call out when you need help.

When I think of how good can come out of bad, it's amazing to see how, for those who have survived rough waters, that experience can become a personal strength. They've gained a new insight, a skill that they can then share with others, showing them the way – teaching them how to get through what they did.

Hopefully, this book provided you with some new tools for learning how to better swim when the waters get rough.

-Paul Shaffer, 2018

Lightning Source UK Ltd.
Milton Keynes UK
UKHW041216061218
333420UK00002B/37/P